To Carol,

The pathway is there for you to explore and enjoy.

With best wishes

Lyn W. Kennole

Other books by the Author
Titles available in The Owler Bar Chronicles
(In reading order):
RuneCrystal
www.angelsintolight.com
angelsintolight@gmail.com

Walking Amongst Angels

Ann W. Kennerley

BALBOA.
PRESS
A DIVISION OF HAY HOUSE

ISBN: 978-1-4525-5878-3 (sc)
ISBN: 978-1-4525-5877-6 (e)
ISBN: 978-1-4525-5876-9 (hc)

Library of Congress Control Number: 2012917580

Balboa Press books may be ordered through booksellers or by contacting:

Balboa Press
A Division of Hay House
1663 Liberty Drive
Bloomington, IN 47403
www.balboapress.com
1-(877) 407-4847

Printed in the United States of America

Balboa Press rev. date: 10/1/2012

Blessed are those who believe
and yet have never seen
John 20:29

To my sister Lynn for her love and support
as the dream finally comes true

Contents

Foreword

This book contains the most important and informative wisdom available today on the realm of Angels. I am very honoured that Ann has asked me to provide a brief Foreword to this, the first of her Angel books.

It is a unique piece of work in which you will be able to share the experience knowledge and energy of someone who has walked this pathway for many years. This book will appeal to all; those who are already well-read on the subject and those who wish to take their first steps to opening the door to 'All that is'. The teachings of Ann, her Spirit Guides and her Angels are focused on assisting you to connect to the world of Angels; how to let them into your life, to love and help you to create a new and joyful existence.

The message from the Angels is a simple one. They are the source of all love and well-being. When you open yourself to this love you open yourself to an abundance of earthly and spiritual awareness and learning. Read these words carefully and allow their guidance to flow into your life. It will change the way you look at your existence now.

The beautiful meditations will connect you to the Angel Realms and their higher energy; gifts to you from the Source, to enhance your life experiences and to fulfil your destiny.

Enjoy this powerful yet most elegant and inspirational book.

Beverley Fairfoull
January 2012

A Gift from the Ascended Masters

Long ago when the light went out and humanity lost its way in the darkness, there followed a time of great sorrow in the Heavens. As the higher energies begin to flow, remember you are a Child of God; a Light-Worker for the planet and for the good of human-kind.

Let your voice be heard, for you have much to do, a lot more to accomplish, as across the lands, oceans and seas your soul's pure-white light shines forth into all the dark corners of the earth. Allow your soul to sense and connect with the vibrational energies of higher consciousness, as you journey back towards God and the light.

The ancient knowledge of your ancestors is being returned to the earth. Now is the time for you to listen with your heart, for there is much to understand; be patient, do not rush; for too long 'we' have remained in the shadows; watching over you, keeping you safe.

The Indigo and Crystal children have already begun their re-birth to the earth; the Rainbow children are following. The mission of these children is to bring peace and to help bridge the gap between our two worlds; with knowledge and wisdom far advanced beyond their young and tender years. As the energies build, let your deep felt love and compassion reach out and touch upon all who are in need of the beautiful blue healing rays, but most importantly have belief in yourself that everything will work out well and for the best, as you embrace and share in the joyful knowledge of these children as you walk into the light.

Children of the Elders how much you are missed, when you journey to the earth, your warmth and love, the sounds of your voices and laughter; also seeing your eyes light up in delight. Remember it all for you have not forgotten.

Go forth and teach, to all who would hear you and listen. Today is the first day of the rest of your life, as you return the ancient teachings of the masters home; where it belongs in the hearts, minds and souls of all the wondrous channels of light here on earth. You are the 'star seeds' from the exalted realm, which will link the chain of life – the chain of light across the planet, as you begin your journey of ascension home.

Permit us the Ascended Masters to bring love and light into your life? Allow God's Messengers the Angels to touch you with the gentle caress of their wings; and know that your Spirit Guides walk beside you.

Remember we will never leave you.

We will keep you safe as we surround you with unconditional love.

Listen to US with your heart

See US with your Soul

And YOU shall know all

Channelled through Ann Walmsley Kennerley
by The Master El-Morya, Chohan of the First Ray
July 2004

Introduction
Where did it all begin?

I've often pondered on that question over the years and especially since the Ascended Master Saint Germaine came into my life.

As a child, I was a natural clairaudient even if I didn't realize it at the time. In my child's mind, I thought the voices I heard in my head were my invisible friends. Over fifty years later, I like to think of myself as a grown up, but there are still child-like qualities about me; for I have a love for all things magical or fairy-like, and friends often describe me by saying "Annie's away with the fairies" or "Annie's the female version of Peter Pan."

Today I know the voices I have heard since childhood and my teenage years, the voices I still hear today, are my Angels or loved ones. The voices are of family and friends who have passed into the World of Spirit.

I grew up sensing I was different from the other children in the neighbourhood. I would know things without knowing how or why I knew. I was aware at that young age of the voices and thoughts in my head. They were talking in the silence, but at the time I thought it was just my vivid and colourful imagination—an imagination that knew no boundaries.

Looking back to my childhood, I think my mother allowed my creativity to soar freely into the universe, all the way to beyond the veil, as I played hide and seek amongst the planets and stars with the friends I had made. Small, slender beings, grey in appearance, with large, black almond-shaped eyes. Years later, they would be brought vividly to life on the television screen and at the cinema.

Many times over the years I have been told by other mediums I've met at various courses and workshops that my mother was a gifted medium. However I have no evidence or knowledge to support this, although I could sense that my mother knew things. She could bridge the gap between the young and the old, and she would make the time to sit and to listen. These are gifts I seem to have inherited from her.

Most Sunday mornings after breakfast was over, my sister Lynn and I would sit at the breakfast table with our mother, and we would debate, discuss, and talk about the different things going on in the world. She would tell us about the stars, planets, and the faraway galaxies and universes where other life forms lived.

I think in her wisdom and because it was so little understood by others at the time, my mother kept my abilities low key. I sense she did this until I was old enough to make my own choices and decisions about the pathway I would walk.

Another childhood memory that has stayed with me is of being twelve years old, which is such an impressionable age, and taking my first steps on the road to self-discovery. As I sat in front of the mirror on the dressing table in the bedroom I shared with my younger sister Lynn, I began to ask the first of the many questions I would ask throughout my life.

Why was I here?

Why had I been born to my wonderful parents?

Why did I have blue eyes?

Why was my hair red?

I was the child with flaming red hair and turquoise eyes, a fact not lost on the matron at Sefton General Hospital where I was born. When my father came to visit my mother and me in hospital for the first time, matron told him that I was the coalman's. She was also heard to quote, "Red hair and turquoise eyes, a rare combination." I was the first redhead born in the family since Great Aunt Honora in the late 1800s. She was my Grandfather Enright's youngest sister and my mother was named after her.

I was thirteen years old, when I was told that I was here for a specific reason but that the reason for my existence would not become evident until the latter half of my life. At the time I did not realize it was one of my Spirit Guides speaking to me. From that moment, I have never called into question what was told to me, nor have I ever argued or disagreed with it. Somewhere in my child's mind, I think I knew the statement to be true and thus accepted the future that was laid out for me.

As I was a painfully shy child, who had been bullied at school, I had little confidence or self-esteem when away from my family and close friends where I felt safe and loved. Memories of my school days are vague and pretty patchy, but it was the best day of my life when I skipped out of the school gate on the last day.

I have never regretted leaving.

I have never looked back.

Sometimes I wonder if Spirit has done this for a reason, and only when my jigsaw is finally complete, will I see the bigger picture and understand why? My childhood, as I've said, is in a great many parts shrouded like the mists of time.

Yet how strange it all seems, as my sister Lynn remembers far more of those early years than I do and will often say, "Do you remember when?" Or "Do you remember this?" Or "Don't you remember that?"

Sadly, I don't.

Although there are a lot of things I don't remember, I know my early childhood memories are filled with an abundance of love, fun, laughter and happiness, and lots of love, hugs, and kisses from our parents and aunts and uncles: Auntie Nell, Uncle Les, Auntie Elsie, Uncle Os, Auntie Annie, Auntie Mary, and Uncle Doug.

Our family didn't have much money. My father worked long hours for the small wage he brought into the house: one pound and ten shillings a week to feed a family of five. With loving, caring parents, my brother John, my sister Lynn, and I grew up in a three bed-roomed terraced house that was filled with family and friends, love and laughter, plus plenty of mischief making, and our paternal grandparents living next door.

I remember little of my father's mother, who died a few months before my fourth birthday. Family members say I am very much like her, and from photographs I have seen, I am inclined to agree, although photos of my mother show I am the mirror image of her. My mother's mother Grandmother Enright died long before my mother met my father, but I like to think that there is a little of each of these three wonderful women within me.

From an early age my mother allowed my soaring imagination and clairvoyant gifts to freely take flight, one day I wanted to be an ice-skater, the next an explorer or astronaut, or even a singer. On other days I wanted to save the planets and stars as I soared across the galaxies beyond the universe to bring back the love and light.

Other childhood memories I remember are the holidays my brother, sister, and I shared with our parents. Every August, for two weeks, we would go to stay with my father's elder sister, Auntie Annie and her husband, Uncle Walter, in Whitley Bay. On the morning of the holidays, a taxi would pull up outside the front door to take us to the railway station and we'd all pile in. The journey from Lime Street Station in Liverpool to Newcastle would take almost ten hours. Father would reserve seats for us, while mother brought along sandwiches, cakes, and biscuits with flasks of piping hot tea.

When the train reached York Station, another train would be waiting at the platform, ready to be coupled behind the carriages. Slowly the two huge steam trains would pull out of York Station and up over the Pennines. If you looked out of the window, at certain points along the track, you could see the two trains with thick white smoke billowing from the funnels. To this day, my love of trains has never diminished.

If I can travel by train I will do so, as the clickity-click of the train on the railway lines returns me time and again to childhood memories, and somewhere along the way my gift of spirit emerged. Even at that young age and taking my first tentative steps on my journey to self-discovery, the knowing was strong within me.

It seems strange that now, in the latter half of my life, the gaps in my memory are beginning to matter. As I sit writing, my thoughts dwell for a moment on what I am writing about, and I wonder if the words forming on the empty pages will keep each of you riveted to the book. So why can't I remember the rest? When will the jigsaw puzzle be completed and the pieces finally fall into place, to reveal why I am here? Many years have passed since that young, sensitive child asked the first of her many questions that would be the forefront of all things still to come.

Today, I am confident and self-assured in who I have become. I can sense within me, a much deeper and a far greater understanding that when I return to Spirit at the end of this life, I will have made a real difference to humanity and to this beautiful planet we call Earth.

As I walk through the latter half of my life, which I call the age of wisdom, my head feels as though it has been filled to the brim and is overflowing with all the information it holds. The golden light, which lies behind my closed eyes, is seeping out, as it seeks a safe haven in which to stop awhile; to take stock of what is happening around me.

When Saint Germaine first came to me in meditation in 2002, I saw a man of great age, with long white hair and beard. His eyes were a piercing shade of blue. In the quiet stillness, he told me across the world, there were hundreds of thousands of like-minded people who like me were eager to learn more about their particular spirituality and to find out about their Spirit Guides and helpers. During the meditation, I was conscious of a powerfully beautiful entity entering my world. I listened as Saint Germaine told me of all the people wishing to make contact with their Guardian Angel, the Archangels, and the Ascended Masters.

He was also quick to point out that the Archangels and the Ascended Masters would be dealt with in the subsequent books he would ask me to write. For now he wanted me to focus and to drive forward the most important thing for humanity; how to connect with their inner-self and spirituality and to build a bridge to the other side.

To-date, if I'm truly honest and after all the excuses and obstacles have been set aside, I'm still no nearer to solving the riddle of where did it all begin than when Saint Germaine first entered my life. Finally, as I put pen to paper and the words are beginning to flow, I can hear them whisper "go back to basics." How many times over the years have I heard those few words, I cannot remember yet each and every time they were said; I would return to my teacher and mentor; though not always eager for the next lesson to begin.

As I listened to Saint Germaine speaking, I could sense and feel the Ancient Master draw close, as he reassuringly told me that everything was in place and I was where I was supposed to be; at this precise moment in time.

He told me the golden key to the Book of Knowledge would be brought forth as the ancient book was opened, and I would begin to understand and learn from the fragile dusty pages. Reaching out through the spoken ancient words, to all whom would listen, of the pathway that humanity would take as they returned back to God and the light; here is where the beginning of my journey of ascension would start.

Friends and especially my best friend Beverley have for a while been encouraging me to write. To write about the knowledge and the wisdom that has been given to me by Spirit and the Angels to put it down on paper, in as much detail as I can remember, thus letting as many people as possible know what the Angel Realms are all about.

What the Ascended Masters are bringing us?

Why 2012 is so important?

The fifth-dimension and what mysteries lie beyond?

Why it links to Atlantis and the 7 Crystal Towers?

Why it all links to the 13 Crystal Skulls?

The inspiration and insight to create and run the Angel Workshops has come from Saint Germaine, my Angels and Spirit Guides; that between us, we can bring a vision of something beautiful, into other people's lives. I hope after reading the book, you will have come to realize and to understand why these beautiful spiritual and angelic beings of light are with you. Why they are also helping me to run and organise the Angel Workshops.

I too am learning the lessons set before me, which will allow me to teach and to pass on; all the wonderful experiences that are to be found on this amazing pathway to spiritual enlightenment and truth; as you connect with the Angels and your Angels connect with you in love and light.

Angels with Wings
God's messengers are bringing closeness to humanity

"You are beautiful, with your transparent ethereal wings of paper torn from the book of dreams. Like the waning and the waxing of the moon and the dawning of the sun, I see you; as you stand before me.

Do you see me?

Or am I just in your dreams?

As you sit on the top of tall buildings or stand on the iron and steel structures that span across the sky; you look across the oceans and lands towards the heavens, as we meet each day at sunrise and again at evening dusk.

Why do you run from me?

Can you not sense my presence as I stand by your side?

If you invite me in, it would only take a second for you to realize that I am there with you. I have all this knowledge and wisdom to pass on but I am tired and worn-out. I am Gabriel with my wings of blues and gold and I can sense that my powerful energy frightens you; as you take your first step into the unknown.

A leap of faith you should not be afraid to take.

Remember how simple it once was.

Trust in me that I will never let you fall; as you allow us to light up the darkness and to bring hope out of the despair. In the Golden Age of Atlantis when peace and harmony existed in the heavens and on the earth; side-by-side, light-worker to light-worker; then over the ages you became blinkered and forgot why you where here. The circle of light and the circle of life have been broken.

What do you think will happen now?

Where do you go from here?

We are here to serve and to protect, as we wait in the wings, keeping watch from afar. We are not the message; we are the messengers of love and light to the earth; that will dwell in your hearts, minds and your souls.

We are close to you.

We are close to HIM.

Look to the heavens and keep watch.

We are on our way."

Channelled through Ann Walmsley Kennerley
by Archangel Gabriel
September 2009

Working with the Angelic Realms

To this day, another of life's mysteries is how I came to be working with the Angels, the Archangels and the Ascended Masters. I first started on the pathway of truth and light in early 1990 as a spiritualist medium and somewhere in-between then and 2001 the Angels entered my life and because it felt right at the time; it all came together.

I remember Saint Germaine's first visit; it was early evening and I was in quiet meditation, in the warm living room of my home, just before I was due to go out to facilitate an Angel Workshop at a local holistic centre. Saint Germaine had entered my life to ask if I would write an Angel book; in fact, to be precise he asked me to write three Angel books. Seated on a wooden bench, he told me he had arranged to meet me there a long time ago.

As the book finally comes together, I hope you will find within the pages a much deeper connection to the angelic hierarchy and you will come to believe in your own Angels as much as I believe in mine. You will learn how to access the knowledge and wisdom that is out there waiting for you, which comes directly from the Divine Source, as you learn how to use these gifts wisely, not only for your own benefit but for the benefit of others, and most importantly of all you will begin to understand what it is all about.

Why you are here?

What is your life purpose?

The Year 2012

Today is Monday, 2nd January 2012. The fifth-dimension and the

Prophecy of 2012 draw closer. It is the beginning of the year that the Mayan Calendar foretold would end on the 21st December 2012; but what lies beyond?

Is this a new chapter in the evolution of humanity?

The year 2011, saw a much faster pace of life; the year simply seemed to have flown-by; as is 2012. Time has been speeded up, so our bodies are ready to access and connect to the higher frequency vibrations, as they help us to adjust and become one with the powerful and faster energies as we move forward into the fifth-dimension.

People who are extra sensitive; mediums and healers have already been particularly affected, as the earth begins its ascension and the higher vibrational energy levels move into planetary alignment. Much has been written about the end of the Mayan Calendar and all sorts of different theories have surfaced. No one including myself can say with any clear clarity or understanding, what will actually happen, as we move into 2013, 2014 and 2015 and the years beyond.

All we can do is to be open-minded and enjoy all that is to come, as the fifth-dimension and prophecy of 2012 lead us into a new era, where life will move at a much slower and more caring pace of life. A place to live, where we will look after one another and help those who are less fortunate than ourselves, without first having to be asked to do so.

As 2012 heads towards its point-in-time all forms of life on the planet will be affected; maybe even changed by the higher energies. Everyone will feel or sense these changes, even if they may not know what is happening at the time, or be exactly sure what it all means. On a deeper and more spiritual level, they will feel something very important is taking place; even if events in their lives do not seem to make sense.

Some people will be affected more than others. It will all depend on where they are on their soul's pathway and journey to self-discovery. They will be touched, changed as human-kind moves towards the transitional shift into the fifth-dimension. The world we know of now is changing as the fifth-dimension comes into its own.

The worlds of air, sea and land are changing, the plants, trees and flowers, forests, the woodlands and rainforests; everything of nature the animals and insects; the planet earth as well. The planetary ascension of the planet has already begun. An ascension that first began long before your birth and is now taking every man woman and child on a journey, into a more profound and spiritual experience of awareness.

After entering the higher consciousness you will find you have passed through the veil; as it is drawn back. You will have changed into much more than you could have imagined or dreamt was possible, as it brings all peoples of different beliefs and cultures together, in harmony and balance; to work for the good of humanity and the planet.

The collective consciousness that was fragmented so long ago is finding unity, allowing the long walk back to the light, truth and Divine Source to begin. Hearts and minds are opening, as the gathering of peoples, across the world; question old beliefs, old systems; the old ways of thinking.

As you strive to make your voice heard, you will say enough is enough, as the realization emerges something very special and important is happening, as the darkness is displaced by the light. Light forces will reach out, as they come together in an understanding, that there is more to this life; than three score years plus ten.

In writing *Walking Amongst Angels*, I ask you bear in mind that the exercises; philosophy and information I am passing on, have been given to me by my Angels and Spirit Guides and thus are my own personal experiences and beliefs.

So as you take a walk with me, through the pages of the book, I hope you will come to understand and accept, what is right for you. What is your own truth?

What the Angels are telling you?

What are they bringing?

What is it all about?

The Angels are helping you to create a brighter and safer world, as they shield and protect you in the higher energies of love and light. Always remember; only if it feels and sits right with your own beliefs and experiences do you accept it as true.

We are only the custodians of this world, the gate-keepers for our children's future. This is our legacy, our gift and the only thing we have to give to the generations of children that are still to be born. With infinite love you can create:

A world of peace

A world without wars or conflicts

No famine or drought – with plenty for everyone

Where people help their fellow-man or woman

A world you can be proud to leave to the future generations

A world where money is no longer needed or used

Where there is no need or desire for materialistic things

A world where 'ego' is no longer needed

A world filled with all that is good for humanity

A world of unconditional love

The fifth-dimension will be a time of quiet reflection:

To a simple way of life

An abundance of health, wealth and happiness

Knowledge will be placed at your feet

A pathway to take you in the right direction

The wisdom to guide your hand and the courage to use it wisely

Since the evening, when Saint Germaine came into my life, many changes have taken place. Some good, some bad, quite a few of them indifferent; but all of them have helped to shape and change me into the woman I am today.

Having spent many wonderful hours in Saint Germaine's company and taken him to my heart, I have kept safe the wisdom of the words he spoke. He wants everyone, to be given the opportunity to read the book, 'so they could learn' about the worlds of spirit and the angelic realms.

The Ancients (the Olden Ones) are entrusting you, with these gifts, in the belief this time around they will be used wisely, not only for your own benefit but for the benefit of the planet and human-kind as a whole.

Bestowing the moral compass of what is just and right, along with the most important lesson that each of us will ever have to learn; how to love each other unconditionally.

The Age of Aquarius has begun

As our souls begin a journey to self-discovery

Into a higher consciousness… the fifth-dimension and beyond

The Hierarchy of Angels

There are said to be 9 Celestial Orders or Choirs of Angels in the angelic realms, depending on which writings or teachings you are referring to. One thing that is very important is that you listen to your own feelings when it comes to making a decision, on what you believe to be true about these realms.

For at the end of day, when all is done and dusted, it simply comes down to what you believe in. To what feels right for you. If you are happy with what you have read, then you accept it as true, but if at any time it does not feel comfortable or sit well with your own beliefs and views, then you discard it and look again.

However, it should be pointed out that there is no concrete proof of just how many Angels or Archangels there are; except that there are an infinite number. Neither do we know with any certainty or clarity what the exact ranking order is, nor the importance of the different angelic groups. After researching the subject on the 9 Orders or Choirs of Angels (in Colossians 1:16) and the rank that they stand closest to God, they are listed below.

The 1st closest to God:

Seraphim
Cherubim
Thrones

The 2nd closest to God:
Princes of the Court of Heaven

Dominions
Virtues
Powers

The 3rd closest to God:
Ministering Angels

Principalities
Archangels
Angels – Guardian Angels

The 1st Order or Choir of Angels closest to God.

Seraphim the Higher Order or Choir of Angels:

Seraphim are the Guardians who stand before God's throne; the 24 Elders who surround the Throne of Grace. The only Bible reference to them is in Isaiah 6:1-7. They are depicted with numerous wings and fiery flames; in colours of blazing reds and gold.

They represent the fire element. Olden writings say that God's grace flows through them down to the Angels. Seraphim keep the balance and harmony in the universe, as they banish the darkness before them.

Cherubim the Second Highest in the Order or Choir of Angels:

Known as the Guardians of God's Laws and the Keepers of the Akashic Records of the Seven Heavens; they were the first Angels to be mentioned in the Bible and are often portrayed with innocent cherubic faces.

In origin they are described, as manlike in appearance and double-winged. Cherubim guard the Tree of Life (Kabbalah) and God's Throne at the east of the Garden of Eden.

Thrones support the Throne of God:

The role of the Thrones is to consider God's decisions and how they can be manifested and brought forth from the world of dreams into the world of reality. They reside in the area of the cosmos, where material form begins to take shape.

They oversee the judgement for each individual's karma as well as humanity as a whole. The lower Choirs of Angels need the Thrones to access God.

The 2nd Order or Choir of Angels closest to God.

Dominions Angels of Leadership:

Dominions are one of the company or rank of angels spoken of in Hebrews 12:22 which have an infinite number. Dominions help to bring teachings and intuitiveness to human-kind. They make decisions and carry out what needs to be done. They regulate the duties of the other Angels and make known to them the commands of God.

Virtues in charge of providing courage, grace and valour:

They are God's forces of love and light and help to create miracles on earth. Referred to as the shining ones, they control the elements and govern all nature; the seasons, the stars, the moon and the sun.

Virtues help those who are having a crisis of faith or belief in God. Working with the Thrones they reward those who face and overcome difficult hurdles or problems in their physical lives. Depicted in war armour and (like the Dominions) they carry a sceptre or sword in their hand.

They also carry a shield for protection.

Powers are the Warrior Angels:

Powers bring the intellect into the sciences: pure mathematics, physics, natural philosophy, astronomy, etc. They create the Professors and Educators in Universities and Higher Colleges. They were the first order of Angels created by God.

The Powers' mission is to defend the cosmos and humans. To fight against the evil spirits who attempt to wreak chaos through human beings. They prevent the Fallen Angels – in the War of the Heavens – from taking over the world and they help to keep the balance and order in the universe.

The 3rd Order of Angels closest to God.

Principalities one of the Celestial Orders of Angels:

Principalities are Protectors of Religion. They are the Guardian Angels of countries, lands, and rulers of nations. Their responsibility is to keep watch over humanity and to help inspire the many leaders of differing nations, so they make wise decisions and the right choices.

The Celestial Order of Principalities brought the courage and strength to the 13 Tribes of the Earth. Another of their roles is to help humanity to keep the faith.

Archangels mean Chief or Leading Angel:

They are God's Messengers to the human race. In the Book of Revelation there are said to be 7 Archangels who stand in the presence of God. They command God's armies of Angels in the on-going battle with the Fallen Angels.

Surrounding the Throne of God they are ready to carry out and pass-on the divine and important decrees to humanity. Archangels are the most frequently mentioned in the bible. 4 of the most recognisable and written about in the Old Testament are Michael, Gabriel, Raphael and Uriel. There is much debate and discussion on the subject as to whom the other 3 Archangels might be.

Names put forward: Camael, Metatron known as Enoch on Earth, (King of the Angels) and Jophiel. Others: Sandalphon known as Elijah on Earth, Chamuel and Raguel, Ariel, Haniel, Jeremiel, Zadkiel and Barakiel. The list is on-going and endless and like the Angels themselves there are an infinite number of names. No one is right or wrong in the interpretation or belief as to whom these mighty Archangels are.

Angels (and Guardian Angels) communicators between God and mortals:

Angels are closest to the material world and humans and they help us to deal with daily matters and communications between humanity and God.

All prayers, messages and requests are answered.

An Angel is assigned to every child at the time of his or her birth.

Angels have the capacity to access any and all other Angels at any time. It has been said in times of grave danger that Angels have been seen clothed in human bodies and have also appeared as an animal. Angels with wings have also been seen. Angels are pure energy of light and love. They reside high above the spiritual world and are not allowed to interfere with the free will of human-kind.

Angels cannot change the direction of the chosen pathway of their charge. Angels will not help humanity to destroy itself nor will they help us to destroy the planet. Angels cannot hurt or harm an individual human being. Angels are the most caring and social and will assist those who seek or ask for their help.

Angels are a powerful force for good; always.

Meditations are placed throughout the book and I hope you will find the time to sit in a peaceful sanctuary with your Angels. A wonderful place to meditate is a bluebell wood. Breathe in the heady scented atmosphere and see the beautiful colours and scenery around you; all mixed in with the wonderful uplifting fragrances of wild flowers in full bloom.

Enjoy.

Meditation
meditate 10–15 minutes – or for
however long you want

1. Make sure you will not be disturbed
2. Light a fragrant candle or joss stick (optional)
3. Sit comfortably
4. Close your eyes
5. Relax breathe gently and deeply

Meditation is a unique and wonderful experience. It allows you to sense and to feel the love and light of your Angels as they draw close to you. With practice you will become aware of their wings around you as they protect and keep you safe. Please read the following meditation slowly and carefully, then close your eyes and as you begin to relax, allow your thoughts to drift.

Walking Amongst Angels

You are walking through a wood which leads to the sea shore. It is warm and sunny. There is a gentle breeze in the air. You feel drawn to the sand dunes at the end of the pathway, gazing at the blue-green sea, you find a quiet place to sit. You scoop handfuls of soft grains of sand and let them run through your fingers. You feel the sand's warmth against your bare skin; above you is blue sky.

As your thoughts wander, your deep breathing slows down. In the silence, you feel calmness, you have never felt before and you become aware you are not alone; at your side is a beautiful Angel of Light. You see colours that have never been seen by the human eye.

A gentle hand touches your arm, as an overwhelming sense of peace, floods through your body and mind. The Angel is dressed in robes of purples and mauves and has rainbow colored wings. Your Angel showers you with unconditional love.

The Angel says. "All you have to do is knock and the door shall be opened. Seek and you shall find. Ask and it shall be given to you."

You know the spoken words contain enlightenment and truth, as the doorway to communicating with the Angels begins to open. In this quiet sanctuary of love and light you sit in the silence; warm sun on your face, you ask the Angel:

Why you are on the pathway?

Where is the pathway taking you?

What are you meant to learn?

Why is the Angel with you?

What does the Angel want to tell you?

You may find that you have several other questions. Please ask the Angel who is waiting to answer them.

Enjoy.

Then: When you are ready

Begin the homeward journey

In your own time

At your own pace

Return to your room

Back to your body

You feel safe and secure.

Reflection

A smile

A thought in the sands of time

Ebbing waves along the shore

Memories; precious like leaves of gold

Never ageing; or growing old

Glistening dew on moist bladed grass

The scent of wet air as it lifts the day

A time for reflection

To a future not yet set

Of where I need to be next

The friendship of laughter

The brightness of a smile; given freely

Quiet strength and purpose

Unconditional Love

Richer; more bountiful than money or jewels

All these gifts; mine

To Give

To Share

Spirit Guides

We all have Spirit Guides who watch over us and help in the good times or in times of trouble as we go about our daily affairs; it's like having a conscience on your shoulder. Although similar to Guardian Angels who also act as our conscience, Spirit Guides have never been Angels.

Who they are?

What do they represent?

Where do they come from?

How can they help you?

Are they family members or friends?

Spirit Guides are not always of human descent. In laymen's terms, some live as energy in the cosmic realm or as light beings of pure white light and love. They work closely with humanity, helping us to evolve. They have a variety of jobs which teach about spiritual truth, knowledge and enlightenment. Spirit Guides are highly developed beings who have chosen to remain close to the earth to help the people there.

Having repaid their karmic debts, Spirit Guides have advanced beyond the need to reincarnate. They have lived former lives on earth many centuries ago; as mediators or teachers, with links to a medium, they are bringing proof of the existence of the soul, once the physical body has died, as they connect you to your loved ones family and friends in spirit. Spirit Guides can sometimes be a native Red Indian.

My main Spirit Guide is Bear Running – a Cheyenne Medicine Man who was my father in a past life. Small in height and slight in build, with grey hair and dark-brown eyes. At his insistence, as he would not take no for answer, he asked my mentor and teacher the late Lynn Brookes to sketch a picture of him, which hangs above my bed in an oval frame. From the spirit world, he watches over me, keeping me safe and after all the centuries that have passed between us; I know I am in safe hands and that I am never alone.

Spirit Guides have been reported as being from other exotic races; this is assumed because of the spiritual existence they have lived or their belief in the afterlife of the soul. Each of you has a main Spirit Guide and many other guides who come and go in your life; arriving for a particular job, a teaching or healing lesson, then when it is completed, they leave or move on to help another soul. Spirit Guides are with you for a reason, a season or a lifetime. Some people are fortunate to have their main guide stay with them all the lives they live.

I first met Bear Running in a development circle, under the guardianship of my teacher Lynn Brookes. I met Lynn in 1990 at Daulby Street, Spiritualist Church in Liverpool and we became firm friends.

As the friendship between us grew, along with my medium-ship; Lynn overtook me and disappeared down the road into the distance. At that point I could have become jealous and wondered quite reasonably why Lynn was moving ahead of me, when I had been on the pathway much longer than she had. There is a reason for everything that happens and on looking back to that time, if Lynn had stayed to walk beside or even behind me, then she would not have been ready; to become my teacher and mentor.

It was at one of Lynn's Tuesday evening meditation groups, that I was given confirmation to a question I had been asking for some time, that was to see my guide Bear Running and even though Lynn had kept telling me that I could see him; I begged to differ I could not.

In the quiet stillness of the meditation, I remember walking down a long avenue of shops. The buildings were tall like the skyscrapers in America and as I turned the corner, I found myself standing at the end of a very long avenue of buildings. Glancing down, I saw a pair of feet a couple of inches in front of my own. The feet were enormous and they seemed to go back the whole length of the avenue, which was a very long avenue. As my eyes travelled higher and higher, I could see a man standing at the other end of the street. He was tall and massively built. (Bear Running had exaggerated his height and size).

Dressed in Indian ceremonial clothing, with full-feathered headdress and war paint on his face, he looked very impressive. His hands and arms were crossed over his chest and he stood with his legs apart. He stood over 100 feet high and was at least 50 foot across in width.

Slowly he bent down; his arms were still crossed, until his face was inches from my own. In a slow drawl he said.

"You can't say that you can't see me now."

As one of Lynn's fledglings; along with Diane, Joan, Jeanette, Audrey, John, Gwen and a lot of other wonderful people, the meditation evenings were a safe haven, where I could get to know Bear Running and learn to trust him; although it would be a little while longer before I actually started to hear him. He has a wry sense of humour, is kind and gentle but can be stern when he has to.

It is not only the spiritual development and growth of the soul your Spirit Guide or guides are helping you with, but with the growth of the physical body as well. Back then I can honestly say it never crossed my mind; I would become a medium. Lynn had to drag me kicking and screaming to the spiritual pathway and the night I tuned-in and connected with Spirit was truly amazing.

In the development circle at my house, which Lynn oversaw, there were nine of us. Joan and I were sitting on the sofa beneath the stairs, the rest of the group on chairs around the room. Closing my eyes, I could hear voices in my mind, giving messages for each person in the group. For the next 30–40 minutes, my mind was filled with these messages, each one going round and round inside my head as I tried to remember everything I had been told. When Lynn finally brought the group out of meditation, she asked Penny to start first and with a smile on her face she left me to last.

It was agonising, each minute seemed like an hour, as I frantically held the information together, so sure I would forget what I had been given, my mind racing with messages going over them time and again.

When Lynn came to me, she was grinning like a Cheshire cat and I felt as though I had been plugged into the electric light socket. I practically fell over my tongue, as the words tumbled out with a whoosh. When I had finished, you can imagine my delight when I was told that the information I had given was correct.

As I looked at Lynn, I saw she was holding her sides with laughter, tears running down her cheeks. She said throughout the meditation Bear Running, whom I had already become aware off, was running up and down behind the sofa, punching the air with his arms and hands as he shouted.

"She's listening!"

"She's listening!"

"She's got it!"

"Oh' boy she's finally got it!"

From that moment, I have heard my guides when they come

to help or to sit and chat. In the quiet times I have to myself, I know my Angels and Spirit Guides are waiting to work with me; as I am to work with them. It is a wonderful feeling to know you are never alone.

Sadly, Lynn passed to spirit in 2004 and I still miss her very much. I miss our talks and the endless cups of coffee in her back room, knowing that I could go to her whenever there was something I didn't understand.

I will always be grateful to Lynn for sharing her life (albeit a short time) with me. As she helped me to see and understand that I could assess the knowledge that was waiting for me but most importantly for opening the doorway to my Spirit Guides. Today, inside my mind, I can still hear her say.

"Trust."

"Don't doubt."

"Go back and ask."

I am constantly reminded of how special she was and Lynn is often with me at the Angel Workshops and as my life journeys towards ascension and my connection to the cosmic spirit of the soul, I have the insight that one woman in particular made it all happen; made it possible; Lynn Brookes.

Lynn and I had often talked of working together in a spiritual retreat and I always thought it would be here in the now. The one guiding factor I have is that Lynn will still carry on teaching whenever it is needed from the other side. A truly gifted medium in her own right, she was a wonderful and inspiring woman; whom I greatly admired and respected. Many fledgling mediums, including myself, have passed through her strong and capable hands to become the spiritualist mediums of today.

Lynn came into my life with unconditional love and a willingness to teach and to give of herself and she asked for nothing in return.

It didn't matter how many times, I asked the same questions, Lynn would patiently go over the lessons to be learnt; from the teacher to the pupil and she passed on the greatest gift of all that she had to give; the teachings of spiritual love and light.

I still miss her. I miss the times spent together, talking, laughing and discussing everything and anything. I miss her smile and her sense of humour. I miss spending quality time with a very special woman I had come to like, trust and love.

I am proud to have called her my friend and more importantly that I was her pupil. I know, she was proud of me because I was one of hers; proud of what I have achieved through her help, teachings and guidance. I think our friendship was unique; friend, mentor, teacher. I feel very honoured and privileged to have walked the pathway with her, even if it was for a short time.

Friendships are so important. They can mean a great many different things to each and every one of us. Spending quality time with those we love has to be the greatest gift of all; trusted friends who will go the extra distance; to the ends of the earth and back for you as you would for them. I once read true friendship was a rare gift, a precious gemstone and if you could count more than three upon one hand, then you were truly blessed. My friends give me unconditional love and support in all I do and I am so lucky to have them in my life.

Each one of them: Beverley, Veronica, Jenny N, Nancy, Peggy, Melinda, Jeni, Ann, the Eureka ladies, Carol and Trevor; all beautiful friends in the truest sense of the word and I know these friendships will always be there, no matter how many miles lie between us. These friendships are what make life truly blessed. It's a sad fact of life some friendships come and go. They are only meant to be there for a moment, a reason or a season and I will always think fondly of them.

It is said we live many life times and each one teaching us lessons: good from bad, right from wrong, poverty or riches, light from dark plus many others. These precious lessons help your soul to grow and one of the reasons you do not remember your past lives or bring them into your current life, is that you have already lived, learnt and grown from those valuable lessons. You can also access the answers to your questions by connecting to the inner-child within.

Meditation is good for the body and the soul. In the silence it helps you to connect and draw close to the Angelic Realms, the Ascended Masters, your Spirit Guides and helpers. In the stillness you can learn how to trust and to develop spiritually in the enlightenment of love and the illumination of light and truth.

As a Rostrum Medium I have a Gate-Keeper who works very closely with me. His name is Jacob. He is my Protector and his job is to keep me safe while I work with my medium-ship. His job is to keep everything in order and to maintain a peaceful ambience and to ensure any problems or confusion is sorted out.

Jacob is not a teacher. His role is to oversee the church services or demonstrations I attend; my safety his primary and only concern.

There are other helpers who will come when you need them. They may not always be obvious but if you listen to your gut feelings you may sense or even realise they are with you. I have always listened to my gut feelings. I have never argued, ignored or tried to change what they are telling me and they have never let me down.

I am often asked how I came to spirituality and why I had chosen this particular pathway. What drives me on in my constant search for answers to all the questions I have asked and the ones that are still to be asked?

Where my unwavering faith, trust and inspiration come from?

To all the above questions and the hundreds more I will probably be asked; I can honestly say with hand on heart, I have no idea.

My spirituality is an intricate part of me.

It is who I am.

Embedded deep within my complex personality they are the endless emotions and feelings that make me tick.

On the subject of how did I get to where I am today, well that's another tale and a half for a start? I feel certain I didn't consciously choose to become a medium but somewhere along the way; I'm equally as certain that I did.

Like Angels, Spirit Guides do not interfere with your free will or force you to do anything you do not want to do. You and you alone are responsible for the choices and the decisions that you make throughout your life, although your Spirit Guides (Angels) will help you where they can. The main role of your Spirit Guides is to let you know your loved ones have survived beyond death; they live on in the spirit world. There is a true saying like attracts like and if you walk in love and light, then only the highest and best from the worlds of Spirit and the Angels will come to you.

Sometimes well known Spirit Guides like Silver Birch speak through others. One such medium was Maurice Barbanell and the words Silver Birch spoke to him of the world of Spirit have been published in a number of books. The following is an extract from the teachings of Silver Birch:

"If you help only one soul to find itself, if you comfort only one mourner, if you heal only one sick person, then the whole of your earthly life is justified. How privileged you are to be aware of the tremendous power that is around and

about you, that enfolds you, guards you, directs you and ensures that you will continue to unfold your latent divinity and the gifts which are your cherished possession." [1]

Ways of communicating with your Spirit Guides:

Clairaudience is a thought-to-thought wave.

You hear and listen to what is being said and then you pass on the messages you have received to the appropriate person. This method of connection is also called channelling.

Clairvoyance meaning *clair* – clear and *voyance* meaning vision.

This is a form of extra-sensory perception with the ability to see visual imagery, people, places, pictures or scenes with your third eye. A clairvoyant is one who sees clearly.

Clairsentient is when Spirit is sensed or felt in the solar plexus region.

This is sometimes harder to do; I know it was with me.

When my Spirit Guides tried an experiment one night at an open circle by taking away my gift of clairaudient, I could feel and sense the emotions swirling around inside me but I couldn't make any sense of what I was picking up. At the end of the evening when Spirit returned my gift of clairaudient they said tongue in cheek.

"Now that wasn't easy was it?"

They were right, but with practice it does get easier.

Communicating with Spirit can be in many ways, depending on what feels right or comfortable with you. The Spirit Guides who watch over you; are here to teach, heal or help you on your physical journey into spiritual awareness. They live on the higher frequency above while we live and experience the physical below.

To quote: *"as above – so below."*

Here are some examples to experiment with. Try each one, or if you prefer use one of your own and see which works best for you.

Meditation:	Say a prayer for protection or guidance
	Make yourself comfortable (music optional)
	Light candle(s) to relax (optional)
	Breathe gently and deeply
	Imagine a brilliant white light above your eyes
	See it getting brighter and brighter as it comes towards you
	Become one with this white light
	Let it fill your entire being
	You are in a place where you feel safe
	Ask the Angel or Spirit Guide to join you
	If you don't connect with your Spirit Guide think of it as an engaged phone line and try again later
Writing:	Write your feelings down on paper
	Write what you want to say to your Angel
	Be clear and specific in your request
	Have a reasonable time frame for getting results
	When you have finished writing burn the paper
	Keep all your written words positive
	The words will be carried into the spirit realms
	All prayers and requests are heard and answered
Talking:	Talk to a person whom you feel will understand what you are sensing, seeing or hearing
	Discuss your thoughts and feelings with them
	Allow them to share their feelings with you
	People of a sensitive nature are drawn to people they feel they can trust

	A two-way street of communication can bring amazing insight
Dreams:	Have paper and pen by your bedside
	As you go to bed ask the Angel to come to you in your dreams
	Ask them to help you remember your dreams when you wake up
	Write your dreams down as soon as you wake; before you forget them

So much has been written on the subject of Spirit Guides you can be spoilt for choice. In your searching of the spiritual world, please remember and be aware there are individuals out there, who are not all they seem.

E.W. Wallis (1848-1914) was a British trance medium, healer, lecturer, inspirational speaker and author. He was said not to favour the idea of Spirit Guides and wrote about his views and opinions. Here's a brief extract.

"That spirit guides were disempowering and
disrespectful to both spirit and the living." [2]

When reading or questioning the many different beliefs and opinions out there, you need to look seriously at both sides of the argument before you come to any decision that might change or affect your views or life-style. If it feels right for you and holds true to your own opinions, beliefs and views; only then do you accept it. If it doesn't feel right, discard it and look again. The best thing about the wonderful journey and spiritual pathway you are walking; there is no need to rush.

Over the years, many people have said that my philosophy is my forte and just before Christmas in 2003 these beautiful words were given to me.

"WE are here to guide you on the spiritual pathway to truth and light. The earth's axis is moving towards the fifth-dimension, a state of higher consciousness. I and the other Angels have been sent by God. We have been entrusted to keep you safe. We are here to teach to all who will listen that:

You are all equal

You are all the same

You are one nation

You are one body of spiritual love, light and truth.

We are bringing to humanity, a deep love of learning, knowledge and wisdom; with the strengths of allegiance, justice and truth. With peace, love and compassion, we will give you the skills that you need and we will help you to rebuild the world in the vision that God created.

You

You whom we love

You do not see us

You do not hear us

You imagine us in the far distant

Yet WE are so near."

Channelled through Ann Walmsley Kennerley
by Archangel Michael
Christmas 2003

Angels and You – A Meeting of Souls
Spiritual Growth and Development

Angels

Angels are found in many religions. Messengers of God, they are sent to do his work. The precise nature and role of these messages vary in the telling. The appearance of Angels is perceived to be a human-like appearance, depicted with wings, long robes and an aura of light around their heads. Earlier concepts of Angels have shifted between a messenger from God or a manifestation of God himself. The 4 most recognised angelic messengers are: Gabriel, Michael, Raphael and Uriel.

For over 2000 years theologians have organised the Angels into 9 Orders or Choirs of Angels. Some hierarchies believed Angels and Archangels to be the only Orders of Angels involved in the affairs of humanity. Passages drawn from the New Testament, Ephesians 1:21 and Colossians 1:16 have tried to establish a Hierarchy of Angels with each hierarchy containing three orders or choirs.

Angels have been here since the dawn of time. To love, to protect and serve you, they bring unconditional love and no matter what you say or do; they will never judge or criticise you. They will never let you down, nor will they leave you or let you fall. Angels help to keep you safe on the pathway you have chosen to walk, and you will never walk the pathway alone.

When I first started to work with the Angels in 2001, I never realized how huge the angel hierarchy was. How far it stretched from our world, the astral into the mental and then the divine called The 7 Planes of Existence.

Within the Angelic Realms, the Ascended Masters reside, also the higher chakras. At the moment healers use 1-7 chakras: red, orange, yellow, green/pink, blue, indigo and purple. As we begin to move through the following dimensions, the higher chakras will come into being:

3rd dimension   1 – 7
4th dimension   8 – 15
5th dimension   16 – 22
6th dimension   23 – 29
7th dimension   30 – 36
8th dimension   37 – 43
9th dimension   the anchoring chakras 44 – 50

There are 3 other dimensions, which cover the 10th 11th and 12th which are the Solar, Galactic and the Universal Body of Light and they will be written about in more detail in Books 2 and 3.

10th Dimension   Solar Body of Light
11th Dimension   Galactic Body of Light
12th Dimension   Universal Body of Light

The Initiation Levels are a part of the higher angelic hierarchy and move from the cosmic physical body –quadrant into the completion of the 7th Dimension. As you explore and search for your own truth, you will find it is a truly wonderful and amazing experience; a journey where you can enter and learn about the cosmic physical plane and the physical and emotional mastery levels. At each stage of the journey you have to take personal responsibility to keep yourself safe as you navigate through the higher energies and realms.

No one else can do this for you and you cannot pass your own responsibility onto another. As you move higher, you will reach the stages of soul merge, atonement to monad and monadic merge levels before finally moving into the beginning and then the completion of ascension.

The final three dimensions and the initiation levels will be dealt with more fully in Books 2 and 3, as will the 12 Mighty Archangels; the 24 Elders who Surround the Throne of Grace; the 12 Elohim: the Creator Gods; the Monad and HUNA Energies that reside in the higher angelic realms then into the cosmic logoic and the divine plane and beyond ascension; all lead you back to the Godhead, the Source; the Creator of Life.

In February 2001, with guidance and help from Stephen my Guardian Angel, Jacob my Gatekeeper and my Spirit Guides, protectors and helpers; the Angel Workshops became a reality. From the moment the flame was lit, these wondrous Beings of Light and many others have worked tirelessly to create in each workshop, a positive secure environment; where a safe and peaceful haven could be sought.

It was a meeting place for like-minded people to come together, make new friends and network socially in a mixture of love and light as communication and laughter flowed freely; all of the above created from the highest and the best of the angelic and spiritual realms.

In quiet reflective meditation, in a peaceful sanctuary, you can gain access to your Guardian Angel, the Archangels and the Ascended Masters, as doorways once closed are now opened. Always remember with faith and belief they are never more than a thought away.

Angels help in many areas of your life, even with the simplest of requests such as traffic lights or finding a car parking space; if you ask for their help they will give it. Which takes me to the time, I was driving into work for an early afternoon Health & Safety Meeting, (at the time, I was working off the main University campus at Aintree Hospital, Liverpool). Driving into the car park behind another car, the thought passed through my mind that it would be difficult to find a space. In fact, after 9 a.m. parking was always a problem at the University.

As I followed the car ahead of me, I saw the driver complete the circuit and drive back towards the main gate. On driving around the circuit, I saw there was an empty space so I nipped in and parked. Looking through the rear view mirror, I saw the driver suddenly brake and get out of his car, scratching his head. I could hear the sounds of giggling in my ear. On asking why they were laughing my Angels said.

"We made him think there was a car already parked in the space so he would drive past and leave the space for you."

As I said; Angels will help if you ask.

There are lots of other ways in which the Angels will help. The name Angel means messenger – messengers from God. Make some quiet time and sit in the silence and ask for their help. It is all there in the universe waiting to be tapped into; an abundance of all that is good:

Problem solving

Help you to find a more challenging and fulfilling career

A house move or find missing objects

Open doorways to fresh opportunities

Help with traffic lights or car spaces

Bring calmer waters where needed

Find ways to help you increase your finances and with relationships

Help you to get to know the inner-child within

Give you the strength and courage to let go of past hurts and harmful relationships

They will bring love and light into your life

The Angel Workshops Take Flight

I have been working with the Angels since 2001, the Archangels since 2002 and the Ascended Masters since 2004. Over the years I have taught many workshops and given talks and lecturers across the North West of England, the Isle of Man and Cobh in County Cork, Southern Ireland and in Europe.

For a long time, I have felt my purpose in life; the reason for my being here is to bring love and light into people's hearts and minds; to share the insight I have been given and if you allow me, to show you the pathway to enlightenment.

As a spiritualist medium, I feel very privileged to work with the Worlds of Spirit and the Angels. The simple exercises in the book are designed to help you connect to the Angels and to learn their names. Allow the Angels to draw close as you come to understand:

Where they are from?

Why they are here?

What it is all about?

In the universe, there is an abundance of love, happiness, knowledge, good fortune and luck. This abundance comes directly from the Divine Source, but with these gifts, you need to be aware of your own personal responsibility.

It is for you to understand and to find out how to access these gifts and why they are so important and that once accessed that they are used wisely. To know why:

The Angels are with you?

How they can help you to achieve your goals and dreams?

What you are here to do?

Why Angels love you unconditionally?

Why you have to invite them in; in the first place.

Angels will help whenever you ask, but remember you have to meet them halfway; the Angels will not bring it to you on a platter, even if it is made of silver. You are probably asking yourself how I go about this. The answer is simple and easy: by asking for an abundance of health, wealth and happiness. It also helps to have an unshakeable belief that you can achieve anything and everything you set your heart and mind on.

You can reach for the stars and fulfil your true potential by bringing your hopes, wishes and aspirations from the world of dreams into the world of reality and making them your own. It is as simple as that by putting this thought into place.

"The art of believing that anything and everything is possible."

You can create your own future in the here and the now by drawing like-to-like-minded people into your life. Bring good fortune and luck; joy and happiness with your creativity and ideas and having positive thoughts and a positive outlook on all you say and do.

People often ask at the Angel Workshops. "Can loved ones who have passed to spirit be my Spirit Guide?" The answer is No. Spirit Guides are guides who are highly advanced. Your loved ones who have passed during your lifetime are not Spirit Guides but that does not mean they are not with you, looking down, guiding and protecting you in times of danger.

Another question I'm asked at the workshops is; "Do I have a Guardian Angel?" My reply is always yes. Even non-believers have a Guardian Angel who watches over them from the side-lines.

Sometimes a person is not aware of or even realizes an Angel is with them because in the grand order of things, Angels have to be invited into your life. That's right; you have to invite them in (unlike Spirit who will bail-in at the first opportunity). This is the vital difference between the two worlds of Angels and Spirit.

I have also been asked. "What will happen if you don't invite them in?" The answer is nothing will happen; your Angel will still stay with you, watching over you from a distance. Angels are bound under the Universal Law of Three. God's Law which governs our world and the worlds around us, the universe and the galaxies beyond and under these laws Angels are not allowed to enter your life unless you invite them in.

Angels exist high above the realms of the spirit world and these wondrous Beings of Light have never walked this world in bare feet. Though in times of great need or when personal danger presents itself, they will manifest in human or animal form in order to save the soul they have been entrusted with. The role of the Angels is to protect, serve and keep you safe, so you can fulfil your potential; they are not your servants. Angels will help to guide and steer you in the right direction, so you become the best you can be.

If you allow the Angels into your life, they will help you to make the right choices and decisions, so that you learn right and wrong; light from dark; good from bad; riches and poverty; to be childless or to share in the joy of children's laughter. All of these precious valuable lessons help to make you a more loving, caring and compassionate person.

Angels are not allowed to change or interfere in the choices or decisions you make on the pathway you have chosen to walk; whether it is good, bad or indifferent. The pathway is yours and yours alone to experience and all that life holds for you and for you to take full responsibility for any outcome that ensues.

In your earthly body, you are helping your soul to grow into the shining beautiful radiating light of energy you are capable of becoming; to become who you truly are. An invaluable part to growth and development, not only for you but for humanity as a whole are the lessons and experiences you undertake to learn, helping you to achieve far more than you ever dreamt or imagined was possible.

To let Angels into your life, you have to listen, to have an open mind and an honest heart. As you allow the energies to flow and enrich your life, you can gain access to the valuable insight that lies within you.

One important question I ask at the Angel Workshops is. "How do you perceive Angels to be?" Responses vary: with wings and halos, wearing long gowns, bare feet; to being part angel–part animal (fish-bird). They can appear without wings, as specks of light or as rainbows in the sky, even dancing rays of light and color; Angels are whoever you want them to be.

A Guardian Angel and other Angels will contact you in ways that make you feel safe and secure, so they may not always show themselves as they truly are. To show you as they really are requires absolute trust on your part.

There is a saying born of this world – but not of this world. I have heard it said many times and it has always given me food for thought, for I know I am of this world – but not of this world. A few tips for when you work with the Angels:

Make an appointment time to work with them
Never be late for your appointment (they have work to do on the other side)
To close down when you finish your work with them
Remember: —
The 3 Golden Rules:

Discipline

Protection

Personal Responsibility

Always remember:

You must never leave yourself open 24/7

Make sure you close yourself down.

Discipline – Protection – Personal Responsibility

The above Three Laws should always be put in place, whenever you work for the World of Spirit.

Church Services (Rostrum)

Demonstrations – Specials

Charity Fund Raising

Spirit Readings / Soul Rescues

Or any other kind of work with Spirit

The First Law is called: Discipline:

In accordance with the Universal Law of Three: Discipline, Protection and Personal Responsibility are put in place when you work with the Angels. They are essential for your safety and to safeguard anyone who might work with you.

Discipline is a very important tool. It is an integral part of the three laws. Without it you would not be able to access the other two and without discipline you might not even be aware of the other two. Discipline is a must when you work with the higher energies and Beings of White Light.

Angels

Archangels

Ascended Masters

The Second Law is called: Protection:

When you work with Angels (or Spirit as a medium or healer) you need to put Protection in place. This second law is an essential part of your work and is very important.

Visualise yourself in white light.

Place it six feet above you and six feet below you.

Without protection negative energies can be drawn to your light and you may feel ill, tired or off-color especially if you work with the higher energies and dimensional realms. Remember to put protection around you and anyone else who might work with/or is involved with you. It is easy to do and can be done using one of the following methods:

Visualise yourself wrapped in a purple cloak

A violet flame cascades down around you

The sign of the cross

The Lord's Prayer

See a pink bubble: decorate it – make it your own

with scented pot-pouri

pink ribbons and bows

a swing to sit on

send love, feel and sense it all

around you

The Third Law is called: Personal Responsibility:

The Third Law is Personal Responsibility and this means that you and you alone are responsible for ensuring you put in place the First and Second Laws of Discipline and Protection. These are your own laws.

Remember you are responsible:

For every word you speak

For every deed you undertake

For each and every action you choose to take

No one else can do this for you

You cannot put the blame elsewhere or onto another person

You are responsible for your own:

Actions   - remember all have consequences

Deeds   - each is a living entity and

        - if sent out negatively into the Universe

Words   - can hurt or harm innocent passers-by

Personal Responsibility belongs to its owner

It cannot be given or be passed to another

The Three Laws are an essential part of the angelic or spiritual pathway you have chosen to walk. Since I began working with my Angels and Spirit Guides they have brought into my life many wonderful and uplifting experiences and I would never have wanted to have missed a moment of it. I know if they ever left me; there would be a huge void in my life I could never fill.

The Laws of Protection and Personal Responsibility are there to make sure you do not leave yourself open 24/7. A soul lives within the physical body that has its own limitations and vulnerabilities. So it is important to make an appointment (ten o'clock in the morning or seven o'clock at night). Or whatever time you have arranged with them, just as they have made time to work with you.

Like our own busy lives and work schedules, Angels have other work to do, so when you have finished you must remember to close down. This can be done with a prayer at the end or if you wish choose your own way to close down using whatever method makes you feel safe and secure:

A prayer

The sign of the cross

A purple cloak of protection

A bubble (in whatever color you choose)

You also open in the same way

Remember:

The Universal Law of Three is there for your protection
and your safety
Use the Three Laws every time you work with the Angels
Please remember to put them into place

Meditation
meditate 10–15 minutes – or for however long you want

Each chakra has its own Angel
1. Make sure you will not be disturbed
2. Light a fragrant candle or joss stick (optional)
3. Sit comfortably
4. Close your eyes
5. Relax breathe gently and deeply

The Chakras of Color – Visualisation:

Imagine you are inside your body at the base of your spine; here you can see the first chakra. It is a beautiful red rose in bud. Watching the bud open *you breathe in the red and breathe out the red.*

Stepping inside the petals, you bathe in the vibrant red energy of light. In the silence a calmness you have never felt before envelops you. You are aware of a beautiful Angel of Light at your right side. You ask this wondrous being their name. When you are ready to begin your journey and the time is right; with your Angel's help you move onto the next chakra; guiding you to a white ladder, your Angel leaves you.

Climbing the white ladder to the orange rose (the sacral) *you breathe in the orange and breathe out the orange.* This beautiful rose chakra is in full bloom, the heady scent intoxicating. Settling in the soft velvety petals you take in the joys of life and all it has to offer.

For a few minutes you can see images and colors that have never been seen by the human eye and you become conscious of another being at your side. A gentle hand touches your hand and as you look up; you find yourself looking into the eyes of an Angel. You feel the presence of peace and unconditional love all around you.

The Angel is dressed in robes of orange, reds and yellows and brings you confidence and self-esteem to take you far on the next stage of your chosen pathway. Leading you back to the white ladder the Angel leaves you.

Climbing the white ladder, you are aware of the higher consciousness of thought that is being brought to you. There is a beautiful yellow rose (the solar plexus) and you see all that there is to see and you begin to understand, as *you breathe in the yellow and breathe out the yellow.*

The Angel of the yellow rose chakra is timeless.

As you look deep into the depth of these ageless eyes, the Angel will help you open the doorways to the chambers of learning and the great mansion halls of knowledge and books. For a while you sit and talk.

When you are ready you climb to the fourth chakra where you see a beautiful pink rose (the heart –love) encased in dark green leaves. *You breathe in the pink and breathe out the pink.* As you sit in the centre of the pink petals you see the glorious colors and finally begin to understand yourself, as the green foliage helps to restore the harmony and balance in your life.

Waiting for you is the mighty Archangel Metatron – King of the Angels. He is the Protector of all the Children of the Earth. Metatron brings great wisdom and knowledge to all who want to listen and to learn. As you become one with this Great Archangel you feel within your heart chakra the love and light he brings to you.

In the stillness you hear a still small voice.

As you continue to climb the white ladder you become more and more aware of your higher self. Your rose throat chakra is the wonderful color of light blue. In the stillness *you breathe in the light blue and breathe out the light blue.*

The light blue chakra is the gateway to communicating with the Angels. Showering you with love the Angel is dressed in robes of silver, yellow and blue. Silently, the Angel steps from the mists to take your hand.

The Angel's wings are the color of rainbows. The Angel has long dark hair and piercing blue eyes and brings love, sincerity and compassion into your life, so that you might share these wonderful gifts with others.

Continuing to climb the ladder you feel awareness all around you; sensing, hearing, feeling, seeing. The vibrations grow stronger. There is a beautiful indigo blue rose (the third eye) and in the stillness *you breathe in the indigo blue and breathe out the indigo blue.*

You sense rather than see the Angel who sits at your side.

Placing a hand on your brow, the Angel begins to open your third eye.

Vivid colors float through your mind as you become one with the world of Angels.

It is time for the final part of your journey as you climb the white ladder. At the top is a beautiful purple rose, your crown chakra the lotus petal. You sense a higher awareness all around you. Vibrations grow stronger as *you breathe in the purple and breathe out the purple* and pure white light envelops you.

There is an ancient Angel at your side, with all knowing eyes and an aura of pure white light, so dazzling you have to shield your eyes with the back of your hand. You talk to the Angel and ask:

Why are you here with me?

What is it that you want me to know?

What do you want me to do?

Why am I upon this pathway?

You feel safe; the Angel will always protect you, as you allow your higher self to emerge

In the quite stillness the Angel begins to impart knowledge Your journey is coming to an end. It is time to return, but you must close each beautiful rose chakra. First the purple - then the indigo blue - followed by the light blue - the pink - then the yellow - the orange and lastly the red. Take your time, move at your own pace, as you slowly descend the ladder through each chakra; close the beautiful rose petals into bud.

Then: When you are ready

In your own time

At your own pace

Return to your room

Back to your body

You feel safe and secure.

Connecting To Your Guardian Angel

As I've already said, one question I'm always asked at the Angel Workshops is: "Do I have a Guardian Angel?" and my reply is yes. Every man, woman and child has a Guardian Angel. This Guardian Angel lives each and every life that you live whether it is for one life or a hundred-thousand; the same Guardian Angel will walk by your side from the moment of your birth until the moment of your death.

My Guardian Angel's name is Stephen. He stands at my right shoulder. He is 8' 10" tall and has huge opaque wings which are tinged with soft hues of purples and lilacs, the edges a silver hue. Dark-brown hair, his eyes are a piercing shade of blue.

Stephen brings with him the Insight and Solomon's Wisdom that I will acquire and use on my spiritual journey through life. The concept of the Angel Workshops was to reach out and to touch each attending participant.

All the Angels ask is for you to have an open mind and heart and to allow your eyes to visualise the wonderful possibilities that are waiting; as you listen to what is being said. Take on board only what you need and discard the rest; without feeling guilty or selfish for having done so.

Guardian Angels are like all other Angels with one exception, they have been assigned to stand by you through your life, through the good times and the bad; your Guardian Angel knows everything about you. Everything you have ever said, done or thought about since the day you were born.

Angels are loyal and loving; they are non-judgemental and will help when you ask them too.

Meditation, lighting a candle, burning incense, creating an altar – are all different ways to contact to the Angels. It is about personal choice. You don't actually need any of the above; all you need to say is "Angel, I need your help." If you open to their energy, you will feel them draw near:

Ask them questions

Let your mind drift – day-dream

Don't try to make it happen

Keep a journal and write about your experiences

With practice you will identify each individual angel by:

Heat or cold

Touch or tingling sensations

Where they stand close to your body

The different energies – size – hair and eye color

Whether the Angel is female or male – tall or small – any distinctive smells

The sound of their voice

Why they are communicating with you

How they can help

Angels have their own specific areas of expertise in which they work. If you don't know or you can't remember the name of the Angel for the job or help that you want, then another Angel will come; if you ask them.

Another question I'm asked is: "Can loved ones already in spirit be my Guardian Angel?" The answer is No. Loved ones cannot be your Guardian Angel although loved ones can be a spirit guardian or guide.

Angels have never been human.

Angel's bare feet have never touched the earth.

They will only take on human or animal form if your life is placed in grave danger or if the danger is serious enough to change the date of your death that you came down to earth with on the day you were born.

We all have a birthday date and a return home to spirit date; the date of our death. Most of us know our birthday date, (though some people due to illness, inherited disease or accident might not know or remember their birthday date).

None of us know our death date.

Your life can be for a few moments, a few minutes or a few hours. You could be here for a set number of years, anywhere from one year to one hundred years, or even three score years plus ten making you seventy.

Your date of death cannot be altered once you have been born.

One of the tasks of your Guardian Angel is to ensure nothing pre-empts this date. Your life is governed by the destiny each of you has to fulfil. If your life was untimely cut-short, then what you came here to do or to learn would not take place?

It could also have a serious knock-on-effect on the other people's lives you might have touched or had an influence on. Hence the reason your Guardian Angel will step in to keep you safe; although they will not interfere or try to change the life lessons you are here to learn, no matter how hard or tough they might be.

The Angel will advise you to take another pathway or not to do something that you know to be wrong but other than that you have to make your own mistakes and learn some of life lessons the hard way. Communicating with your Guardian Angel is not difficult; there is nothing magical about it. Angels are not allowed to interfere in your life and will not offer to help you unless you asked them to (except in times of physical harm or grave danger).

There are many ways in which you can communicate with your Angels; all you need to do is call them.

The Guardian Angel meditation I use in the Angel Workshops is easy to follow. Don't worry if you don't get a name the first time. Look on it as an engaged telephone line and try again later. Sometimes the best things in life are worth waiting for; worth fighting for and this easy to follow exercise allows you to draw close to your Guardian Angel and to invoke his or her name. Please be mindful the name may be an everyday name; for not all Angels have biblical-sounding names.

When I was given the name Stephen I must admit to feeling quite disappointed and upset and boy did I show it; for quite wrongly I had assumed his name would have been a biblical-sounding name. Anyway, I felt this huge presence beside me and I could feel the Angel drawing himself up to his full height and I heard a quiet but firm voice say.

"What might I ask is wrong with Stephen?"

Stammering and spluttering that there was nothing wrong with Stephen, I suddenly felt very ashamed of myself. The following day on going into work I asked for confirmation of his name. During the course of the day it came three times.

The first confirmation was when a work colleague asked if I wanted to read a book she had finished. I said yes; the book was called "The Talisman"' by Stephen King; the second confirmation was from a Pharmaceutical Company Rep; Mr Steven Thorn-Bourne and the third a Mr Stephen Wentworth, Consultant Anaesthetist who had made an appointment to see my boss.

That day I was given 3 white feathers.

What more proof did I need?

None.

Meditation
meditate 10–15 minutes – or for
however long you want

Opening the doorway to find the name of your Guardian Angel
1. Make sure you will not be disturbed
2. Light a fragrant candle or joss stick (optional)
3. Sit comfortably
4. Close your eyes
5. Relax breathe gently and deeply

Invoking the Angels

The Invocation is spoken out loud. The power is increased when the invocation is voiced three times. This increases the power in accordance with the Universal Law of Three and is known as the Power of the Names and the Number Three.

You ask the Angel for their name three times.

Guardian Angel; please can give me your name

Guardian Angel; please can give me your name

Guardian Angel; please can give me your name.

Then you ask the angel to be with you as you complete your Invocation by saying the following words:

Guardian Angel, Guardian Angel, Guardian Angel

Please be with me now

In Love and Light, In Love and Light, In Love and Light.

Remember: Trust and Intent

Show your intent is honest

During the following days, ask for confirmation of the name you have been given. If the name of your Guardian Angel is correct, you will receive confirmation; a sign, a symbol or a message. These can come in lots of wonderful ways:

You may be told his or her name in a dream

See a billboard or poster with the name on it

Borrow or buy a book and see the title written on a page

See a film

Find a white feather; a sign an Angel is with you

If you say the name you have been given out loud and then switch on the radio, you may hear a song with the name in it

Other ways the Angels will make contact to let you know they are with you:

White Feathers: Can indicate an Angel is with you

That you are on the right pathway

If you find one feather the Angels may send you two more –total 3

Colors or lights: In meditation ask the Angels for help

You may see lights or shooting stars

The colors: purple, blues, greens, yellows, gold, pinks, silver, white may appear in your mind

Fragrances: You might smell a familiar fragrance or scent

You may smell it time and again

This can often signify your Angel's approval

Tingling: As you ask your Angel for support you may feel tingling in your hands or body

Try calling in another Angel to see if the tingling increases or changes

Feelings of loving warmth: As you allow the Angels into your life you may feel emotions of love and trust

The feeling of warmth and peace

Your palms may feel warm or ice-cold

You feel deep love in your heart

If you allow them Angels will bring you pure unconditional love and they also have special ways in which to send you their messages or respond to your prayers and invocations, which indicate their presence in your life.

White Feathers

For those who don't know, it is said if you see a white feather on the ground, it is a sign your Guardian Angel is watching over you. Finding a white feather is a way for the Angels to say they are with you or near you.

White feathers can be left in response to your prayers and requests that are sent to the angelic realms. All prayers and requests are received, heard and answered. White feathers often signify they are bringing guidance and that all will be well in your life.

More often than not the feathers you find will be white ones but Angels have been known to leave colored ones. People are more aware of Angels in their lives and feel and sense their presence as the Angels draw close. The veil between the two worlds is being drawn back, allowing the closeness and the connection to take place.

I remember the time when a Circle of Light evening was held at a Spiritualist Church I attended. In the morning when the cleaners went into the Church to tidy up, they said they found the floor covered in feathers of every color imaginable. Feathers can appear on the ground or floating in the air. I once found a white feather on the bonnet of my car.

It was lying completely still, even though a hurricane type wind was blowing, it never moved an inch. I also found a white feather in the car door, although when I had left the car, having closed and locked the door behind me, no feather had been there, but it was there on my return.

I was given a beautiful white angel feather that fell to my living room carpet while I was reading an Angel message. Angels will use different ways and methods to get their messages across, to let you know they are near and are there to help and you are not alone.

Throughout earth's history, many cultures and beliefs have used or seen feathers, as being of spiritual or even magical origin; there are many different textures and colors to the feathers and represent anything from literal to legendary.

Feathers can have symbolical meaning for spiritual evolution and the eventual ascension to a higher plane. They were worn by native American Indians symbolizing communication with their Spirit Guides, expressing celestial wisdom; the power of thunder, the air and the wind.

In Celtic tradition feathers were worn by the Druids in ornate feathered robes. These robes were worn in ceremonies to invoke and gain insight and knowledge.

Ancient Egyptian mythology and early Christianity believed that feathers had symbolic meanings. The Egyptians would pray to Ma'at the Egyptian Goddess of Justice.

Early Christians said feathers represented virtues. An image of three feathers was made into signet rings, with each feather symbolising faith, hope and charity. In dreams feathers can represent travel and the ability to move freely in life. White feathers can indicate innocence, or a fresh start and new beginnings on the spiritual pathway. White feathers are a symbol for truth, light and love or for wisdom, knowledge and ascension.

Meditation
meditate 10–15 minutes – or for
however long you want

Opening the doorway to the Archangels
1. Make sure you will not be disturbed
2. Light a fragrant candle or joss stick (optional)
3. Sit comfortably
4. Close your eyes
5. Relax breathe gently and deeply

Imagine yourself in White Light.

Speak the Invocation:

The power of the invocation is increased when voiced three times. This power is increased in accordance with the Universal Law of Three. If you know the name of the Archangel you want to draw near to you, speak their name out loud.

Gabriel – Raphael – Sandalphon – Michael – Metatron

(or whichever Archangel you wish to contact)

Complete the Invocation by saying e.g.:

Archangel Gabriel

(or the Archangel's name you wish to connect with)

I ask you to draw near

In Love and Light

Let me feel your loving warmth

(voice the Intent x 3)

Remember: Trust and Intent

Show that your intent is honest

Archangels of the Zodiac

There are 4 Zodiac Archangels:

Archangel Raphael is the Healing Angel:

Raphael represents the air element and he governs the zodiac signs of Gemini, Libra and Aquarius. He helps to bring harmony and cleaning or cleansing into your life, as he helps you to de-clutter specific needs or areas. He oversees spring and the eastern hemisphere. His colors are blue, gold and yellow.

Raphael is the Keeper of the Holy Grail and he speaks to you through your higher mental abilities and awakens you, if you allow him, to an inner sense of your own creativity and beauty.

Archangel Michael is the Champion of Justice:

Michael represents the fire element and he governs the zodiac signs of Aires, Sagittarius and Leo. He brings protection, strength and balance; overseeing the season of autumn and the southern hemisphere. His colors are red, pink and purple.

He brings patience, inner-strength, and protection against psychic imbalance and danger. Guiding you along the pathways of llfe, Michael will help you to let go of the old and the past, enabling you to let in and build the new.

Archangel Gabriel is the Angel of Revelations:

Gabriel represents the water element and he governs the zodiac signs of Cancer, Pisces and Scorpio. Gabriel brought to Mohammed the Book of the Koran which took place over 40 years until Mohammed's death in 642. In total Gabriel gave Mohammed 666 verses.

He told Joseph of the birth of Jesus Christ and spoke to John the Baptist. He oversees the season of winter and the western hemisphere. His colors are emerald, sea green and turquoise. Gabriel is the bringer of hope, illumination and love.

Guardian of the Sacred Waters of Life, Gabriel gives you a greater understanding of your Inner-Self the child within. Speaking to you in your dreams and intuitive teaching; he brings illumination into your life and soul.

Archangel Uriel is the Regent of the Sun:

Uriel represents the earth element and he governs the zodiac signs of Taurus, Virgo and Capricorn with alchemy, wisdom, vision and peace. He represents the summer season and the northern hemisphere. His colors are white, fawn and brown (all earth tones). Uriel is said to be the tallest of the Archangels with eyes that see across Eternity.

He works within the Diva, the Planes of Existence as he helps and assists the nature spirits to create harmony and balance within the kingdom of humanity. Allowing Uriel into your life will open the doorways to the Fairy Kingdoms.

If you believe in re-incarnation, then the following chapter on the mighty Archangels will hopefully begin to make sense and for those of you who don't believe: I hope that one day you will find your own pathway to walk; as you come to understand, where you are from and why you are here.

The Mighty Archangels
Gabriel – Raphael – Michael – Uriel
Chamuel – Jophiel –Raguel

Guardian Angels and Archangels differ in one very important aspect, in that each and every person's life the Guardian Angel lives every life-time that they live.

The Archangels' role in your life is significantly different, as they are governed by the signs of the zodiac, so the Archangel will change with each life-time you live. If you could predict you would have the same birthday; the same day and month in each life you've lived; then you could all make a killing at the bookies.

One of the main tasks of the Archangel is to oversee the passage of the soul at the moment of birth. He travels down with the soul to make sure it reaches the child and is born safely and once the soul has connected with the child; the Archangel will step out of the child's life onto the perimeter, allowing the Ministering Angels to draw near.

It is the job of the Ministering Angels, to watch over the child as he or she grows from infancy to adolescence and then into adulthood. As the child becomes an adult and thus capable of making his or her own decisions and choices, the Archangel will return and will walk the rest of the pathway with you until you return to Spirit. Another role of the Archangels is to help your soul to grow and develop.

There are many people of different faiths or beliefs and others who do not believe in a Divine Source or who use another name for the Creator. There are people who do not believe in an afterlife or that God is within us all.

In writing *Walking Amongst Angels* the faith and belief I talk about in this paragraph, is from my own religious upbringing in the Methodist Church and from my own personal journey; as I walk this wonderful spiritual pathway.

All archangels' names end with 'el' meaning in God. Angels can be in many different places at the same time. Like the belief in a Divine Source that God lives within each and every one of us at the same time.

The 4 Archangels most people know are:

Raphael   – The Archangel of Healing

Michael   – The Champion of Justice

Gabriel   – The Angel of Revelations

Uriel   – The Regent of the Son

The above 4 Archangels were depicted in the Christian Bible, although the names of the other 3 Archangels can differ and are open to much debate and discussion.

The Christian Church, Pope Zachary (8th century), in 745 A.D. ordered 7 Angels to be removed from the ranks of the Church's recognized Angels; 2 of these Archangels were Uriel and Raguel. The reason for this remains unknown.

Whether you believe it or not, heaven is very organized, and it may surprise you to know all heavenly beings have a specific job to do. The Archangels each serve on a certain ray (aspect of God) and have spiritual retreats and homes in the etheric realms (heaven-world) above certain powerful countries and places on earth.

If you say their names out loud they will come into your life.

If you call them 3 times first thing in the morning; it should set you up for the day.

I hope what you will learn from this book is there are many Angels and Archangels in the angelic realms. There are many different opinions, ideas and views as to whom these mighty Archangels might be.

The following chapter covers some of them and I believe no one is right and no one is wrong in the naming of these wondrous Beings of Light. The following Archangel names were given to me in quiet reflective meditation.

The Mighty Archangels

Barakiel: is called – *the Lightning of God.*

He sits at the right hand side of God. Granting success, fortune and excellent luck to mortals, he inspires fun, joviality and a sense of humour.

Tall, slim, a strong Angel, he is firm but fair, with silver tipped wings; he has dark-brown hair and blue-eyes. The Prince of the 2nd Heaven, Barakiel is the Angel of February. He is also the Ruler of the planet Jupiter.

Camael: his name means – *he who sees God.*

One of 7 truly powerful Angels he stands in the presence of God. A teacher and mentor he has a deep love for humanity. He wears robes of silver, blues and reds and stands over 9 feet tall. Well built and powerful, he is dark-eyed and dark-haired.

He is the Ruler of the planet Mars and one of the governing Angels of the 7 planets.

Sandalphon: (Elijah) the Prophet Elias.

Sandalphon is the Archangel who oversees the Astral Plane of Existence (our world) under Lord Maitreya in the Office of the Christ. He is said to be the twin brother of Metatron. Sandalphon is a very tall Angel with gold wings, fair hair and brown eyes. He wears robes of sea-greens and blues.

He is the Ruler of the 6th Heaven and the Chief of the 7th Heaven.

Barbelo: is an Angel of abundance –plenty.

Barbelo stands within the Dominion Order of Angels, the 2nd closest Order to God. She represents faith, goodness and integrity. Pray to her to fill you with these gifts and virtues. Slender and graceful, with opaque wings that are tinged with soft pinks and peach, she has fair hair and green-eyes. She is feminine, gentle, kind and caring.

A Teacher of the Souls; Barbelo brings open-mindedness.

Dina: an Angel who works closely with human-kind.

Dina inspires mortals to pursue a love of information and understanding, through teaching and learning. It is said when the world was created; Dina taught to humanity 70 languages. He is said to be older than time, small in height, well-built, with salt-pepper colored hair. He is loyal and caring, and can be formidable if put to the test.

Dina is the Guardian Angel of the Law.

He dwells in the 7th Heaven.

He is in the 3rd closest Order of Angels to God.

Azrael: his name means – *whom God helps.*

His job is to keep track of the dying. He records the births and erases the names of those who have died. He helps people to cross over to Heaven. He wears a dark hooded robe and carries a scythe. Tall and powerful he has 4000 wings. He helps humans to assimilate on the other side.

Azrael is also known as The Angel of Death.

Ariel: his name means – *Lion of God.*

Ariel is involved with the healing and protecting of nature and he works closely with King Solomon in conducting manifestation, spirit releasement and divine magic. Descriptions may vary. At times he is placed among the fallen angels; routed by the stern obedient seraph Abdiel during the War of the Heavens.

Ariel is the Ruler of the Winds.

He is one of 7 Princes who rule the waters.

Haniel: his name means – *the grace of God.*

Haniel uncovers lost secrets. You can call on this Archangel if you need to speak in public. Allow him to bring beauty, harmony and loving friends into your life. He was the Archangel who escorted Enoch to the spirit world; where he was transformed into the Angel Metatron.

Dressed in robes of beautiful purples and reds, he is a tall angel who stands over 10 feet tall with silver wings. Haniel is slender in build and muscular.

Haniel is the Angel of December.

He is also the Prince of the Angelic Orders of the Principalities and Virtues.

Metatron: is the King of the Angels.

He occupies the throne next to the Divine throne. Nothing happens in our world without his knowledge or consent. He has thousands and thousands of midrad eyes, all seeing, with 48 pairs of wings. he is powerful and stern.

After the Exodus Metatron led the children of Israel through the wilderness into safety and continues today to lead them both on Earth and in Heaven and helps them to adjust after crossing over. Tender and loving with children he will protect and guard them fiercely.

Metatron is the first (as also the last) of the 10 Archangels of the Briatic World.

He is the Angel of the Covenant.

Metatron is the Chancellor of Heaven.

Raziel: Secret of God – 1st closest Order to God.

Raziel helps you to understand esoteric material, manifestation principles, sacred geometry, quantum physics, and the higher levels of psychic abilities. He also assists with alchemy, clairvoyance and divine magic. Small in height but huge in stature, his hair is white and he has shrewd blue eyes that miss nothing.

The Angel of Mysteries, he works miracles. Some say he is: Older than Time. He Wrote - The Book of the Angel Raziel – wherein all celestial earthly knowledge is set down.

Zadkiel: (also known as Sachiel) his name means – *Righteousness of God.*

He brings joy, mercy, forgiveness and compassion to humanity and has a kind gentle presence. Dark haired and blue eyed; he is robed in dark blues and silver. Strong and powerful he has numerous wings.

Zadkiel holds the Office of the 7th Ray and the Violet Flame.

He resides in the Order of Angels known as the Dominions.

Bath Kol: *(Bat(h) Qol* she stands left of God's Throne – 1st closest Order to God.

Is a wonderful Angel who encourages truthful communications and prophecy, she also grants insights into the future (where appropriate). She is small with dark hair and large beautiful green eyes. Fiery and stubborn she doesn't suffer fools gladly. She is compassionate with an abundance of awareness and perception.

Bath Kol is a Holy Guardian Angel with a heavenly voice and she receives communication from the Ancients.

Jophiel: known as – *the Wise One.*

Is the Angel of Beauty and Illumination, the Angel of Paradise? Jophiel will help you to absorb information as you study for/or to pass your exams. Her energy helps you to slow down and to smell the roses. Radiant and beautiful, she is tall and slender. Her yellow rays bring a fresh approach to life, enchantment and pleasure. She works tirelessly for humanity.

Jophiel has a retreat: over the Plains of Central China, south of the Great Wall near Lanchow.

Chamuel: known as the Loving One – *He who sees God.*

Chamuel brings love, compassion, mercy, creativity and forgiveness. He helps to find lost things and is a whiz at improving communications between people with relationships either personal or professional.

Writings say he is clothed in gossamer pink robes but in fact it is the layers of pink light that people see.

He is the Archangel of the pink ray of divine love.

His retreat is over the City of St. Louis in Missouri, USA called the Temple of the Crystal Pink Flame.

Metatron is one of only two Archangels whose name does not end in 'el'. One of two Archangels who were human before becoming Angels (his brother Sandalphon/Elijah was the other). On earth Metatron was the Prophet and Scribe Enoch.

A lot of information has been written on the Archangels and the Angel Realms. Go and dip your toes in the water, paddle about and explore; have some fun, as you learn more than you could ever have imagined. Angels love music and they will come to you, if you play your favourite songs or classical music, pop or jazz. They also love to dance, so empower the rest of your life, by inviting your angels into it. Sing and dance with them; as they bring you wonderful inspiration and enlightenment, joy and laughter love and light.

The Angels will assist whenever you need them as they help you to develop your intuition, inner wisdom and insight. They have no gender and can appear as male or female; tall or small; fair or dark. Or in whatever shape or form the person they are connecting with feels safe.

If the descriptions and attributes on the previous pages seem different from what you have read elsewhere, then trust in your own intuition and gut-feeling. Is it right for you? If it doesn't feel right or sit at ease with your own beliefs, then discard it and search again, for your true north compass is still out there waiting for you; along with a wealth of information for you to acquire.

A great deal has been written about the Angels in books and on the internet and at this point or stage in the equation, is where your own personal responsibility must come into play. You must only accept what feels right for you.

In heeding the words of Gautama Buddha, remember to accept only that which you believe to be true and to listen to your intuition on the spiritual pathway you walk.

"Do not believe in what you have heard; do not believe in traditions because they have been handed down for many generations; do not believe in anything because it is rumoured and spoken of by many; do not believe merely because the written statements of some old sage are produced; do not believe in conjectures; do not believe in that as a truth to which you have become attached by habit; do not believe merely on the authority of your teachers and elders. After observation and analysis, when it agrees with reason and is conducive to the good and benefit of one and all, then accept it and live up to it." [3]

Heed the words of Gautama Buddha
Spoken 2600 years ago

Meditation
meditate 10–15 minutes – or for
however long you want

Archangel: Tzaphkiel is the keeper of the Akashic records
1. Make sure you will not be disturbed
2. Light a fragrant candle or joss stick (optional)
3. Sit comfortably
4. Close your eyes
5. Relax breathe gently and deeply

In the silence of White Light

Allow your inner thoughts to drift into an ocean of deep blue

Feel yourself connecting to your Higher Self

As Yin Energy moves around you

The Divine Name: Yhvh Elohim is called, meaning (Lord God)

The Cosmic Mother touches your soul

Pure love and compassion are a part of who you are

Fragrance of lily and frankincense lifts the air

A red rose is given with love

In the quiet stillness a doorway is opening

You ask for the Wisdom of Solomon

Feel the loving energies of the Archangel: TZAPHKIEL

– as tingling sensations surge through your body

In this safe haven you become one with the Archangel

Then: It is time to say goodbye

Slowly return to the room

Back to your present surroundings

In your own time
At your own pace
Open your eyes
You feel safe and secure.

Autumn

Again the autumn leaves drift down
Under the glow of the amber sky
They float and dance like whispering winds
Unfolded; browning like death's wing
Memories caught against the breeze
Not forsaken in nature's theme

Angel Stories

Over the years, at the Angel Workshops I have taught, I have met many lovely and beautiful people; all of them at different levels on their pathway of enlightenment and truth.

In correspondence, they have sent me over the years, some have shared the wonderful encounters and experiences they have had with their Angels; seeing, hearing, sensing or quite simply how Angels have changed their lives for the better.

The following stories are from friends and some of the wonderful people I have met who have encountered their own Angels. They have given permission for me to share these incredible memories, extraordinary experiences and stories with you; in order to let you know you are not alone with your own Angel encounters and experiences.

"This is a tough one, Ann because I see Angels as well as Spirit. I have seen Archangels on several occasions and had Archangel Michael lay across my bed one morning, with his powerful sword lying by my side. I have seen Angels, guarding my house, huge Angels around me, where the body of the Angel was upstairs and the legs downstairs. I have had many experiences with Angels and I guess I am blessed to see them. In many of my readings, I will always see an Angel or two. The Archangel Barakiel has spoken to me on several occasions. When he sifts his energy through me from that great height, I hear his voice, loud and clear, giving me inspiration as he tells me things.

His voice can fade very quickly then it comes through, in the thought, that he has a very deep voice.

I have had the Archangels Michael, Gabriel, Raphael and Uriel stood around me when I have asked them for protection. I have seen them near solid. I felt safe with them, but I did think at the time, it was for protection; to show me in general that they are always here for me when I ask for protection or that something was about to happen. Well on that night, it was a woman. I'm guessing she felt some jealousy and was causing trouble for me. Then I saw the Angels appear around me again, and my Dad's voice came out of my mouth to stop this woman in her tracks, and it did. I was told by my Guardian Angel that they protect their light workers from others who are trying to stand in their way, or interfere in their mission. It gave me a lot of upliftment, to know how close they are to us all.

I am really pleased to hear you are writing this book. I know you have been planning to write it for a while. I hope this helps in some way and wish you a very successful 2012, lots of love and light."
Jeanetta Ogden
Warrington, Cheshire – 2011

"Angel sighting while sitting in what I call 'the spiritual chair' (because of the number of Spirits I regularly see when I sit in this chair) in my living room one cold but sunny morning having just enjoyed a cup of tea, I felt a bit tired and was just dozing when I opened my eyes and just for what must have been a second saw what I know to be an Angel.

The light from the window was bright and the Angel was misty white but transparent and at least 8 foot high which is the height of my ceiling. I did not see the Angel's face which I felt might have been through the ceiling but did notice that the thickly feathered closed wings were nearly down to the floor the Angel was enormous. There was no dialogue and the Angel had with him a more life size spirit of slim build also misty white and transparent but with clearly visible dark hair and I felt this could have been my late husband. They disappeared in seconds and I shouted 'come back' but they never did.

I do hope to see them again sometime and wondered why I had been privy to this apparition; maybe it was to convince me that there are Angels helping us all the time; was the Angel bringing my late husband to me or was my husband bringing the Angel to me knowing I needed his help and reassurance at the time I feel this is much more likely. I felt privileged to have seen them, if only for a second or two, and just wish I could have held the vision longer. I felt very emotional afterwards and still feel humbled and comforted by the experience.

I have come across many human Angels on my journey and I feel these people are put on my path for a reason as well. I am much happier since I started on my spiritual path and trust my intuitions much more than previously. If spirituality has taught me anything, it is what little I know and what a lot I have to learn and experience Wishing you lots of love and light."
Pauline Oliver
Southport, Merseyside – 2011

"I am a friend and work colleague of Ann's and we share a love of Spirituality. I am learning to develop my mediumship skills, whilst Ann's are truly developed. I was lucky enough to attend one of her Angel Workshops last year which I really enjoyed and through Ann's help was able to meditate and find out the name of my Guardian Angel.

Ann you are a charismatic lady and have a magnetic aura. You are wonderful company and I feel lucky to have you in my life."

Ann Furlong
Widnes, Cheshire – April 2008

"I write as a lifelong friend of Ann, who I have had the privilege of knowing for over 30 years. From childhood, Ann has known that she would tread the spiritual path, not just for herself, but to light the way for others and to guide and teach those who wish to explore the sacred and angelic realms.

Ann has devoted her life to drawing the spiritual and earthly worlds closer together. Her warmth, calm and inner wisdom have for many years, uplifted and inspired others to share her dreams and embrace the spiritual life.

She has much strength, in particular her enthusiasm and energy, which are infinite, as her many friends and colleagues will confirm. Ann's Angel Workshops showcase her remarkable knowledge and have been spectacularly successful. Many more are planned, and as she is also a writer of many years standing, her teachings will, I'm sure, soon become available to an even wider audience via the written word. Ann is without question an outstanding teacher and mentor in the spiritual community and a potent force for good in this materialistic, pressured world.

She is a unique lady who stands at the gate of our earthly reality, drawing back the veil to reveal the realms beyond our own. Ann walks the true path of love and light. May radiance of the Angels always shine upon you, Ann."

Your friend,
Beverley Fairfoull
Warrington, Cheshire – February 2008

"I first met Ann Walmsley Kennerley a few years ago when she came to the Isle of Man as a visiting medium at the Christian Spiritualist Church. She is a warm, open and honest person, well respected and admired and an excellent medium.

Ann is a kind and generous lady with a positive outlook and a sharp yet gentle sense of humour. She is always willing to see the best in everyone and to trust and love unconditionally. Her capacity to share her knowledge, love and wisdom has no limits. I feel honoured to have such a wonderful friend as Ann.

I would highly recommend her workshops and courses as she is a fountain of knowledge when it comes to the Celestial Angels and the Ascended Masters. Ann is a very gifted teacher and I have learned a lot from her, seen and experienced her, gentleness and understanding as she brings out the best from those attending her workshops and courses.

The world needs more people like Ann to show us the way forward through life on our spiritual pathway, to work in love, light and truth when working with those higher beings of light."

Val Crowe
Isle of Man – January 2008

"My name is Paul Martin and I attended Rock Ferry Spiritualist Church on the Wirral as the Healing Group Leader responsible for the training and development of up to 8 trainee healers at any given time.

I have known Ann Walmsley Kennerley for more than 5 years. She has attended our church at regular intervals over this period of time as a medium providing wonderful evidence of the spirit and its loving support.

Ann has also provided Angel Workshops to church members, which were well received and enjoyed by all. I also joined an Angel Workshop, which Ann provided and had a wonderful experience connecting with my 'Spirit Guides' and the angelic realms through their wonderful and powerful energies.

I have always been impressed with Ann's enthusiasm and her unselfish approach to the needs of the group when they experience her workshops, taking time to explain the connection to the energies and the various levels that can be achieved.

I am looking forward to reading the children's book Ann completed recently and to reading any of her forthcoming Angel and Spiritual books for guidance. I wish you well Ann, on your continued spiritual journey, in Loving Light and Truth."
Paul Martin
New Ferry, Cheshire – January 2008

"Ann. You are lovely! Thanks for the wonderful insight and beautiful experiences. Stay safe. I wish you happiness, warmth, love and light."
Manny Emslie
Frodsham, Cheshire – April 2008

"Ann. Thank you for all the work you have done with us."
Kate Lloyd – April 2008

"I have really enjoyed this workshop and am going to miss you.
With love and light."
Lorraine Ellis – April 2008

"Many thanks for the hope and joy you have given to my friend Jayne at the Angel Workshop she attended. I hope to meet you myself very soon. Blessings of Love and Light."
Lainee
Wirral, Cheshire – June 2006

"Hi Ann, I have read with great interest your website. I have printed off your profile and newsletter etc. very interesting. I cannot wait for Saturday when we meet to discuss the Angel Workshop programme. I have believed in and seen Angels all of my life."
Nancy May Foster
Ellesmere Port, Cheshire – February 2005

"To Ann, May you be touched by the sweet thoughts of Angels? This is the best Angel Workshop ever. Wishing abundance, love and magic."
Peggy Frahill and all the gang at Rainbows End
Cobh, Co. Cork, Ireland – December 2004

"Hello, I was at your workshop in Cobh, Co. Cork, Ireland on Saturday, 4th December. I was visiting my sister for a break. I attended the Angel Workshop with an open mind.

I enjoyed the experience, particularly the meditations. I am still trying to find out the name of my Guardian Angel."
Olive Johnson
Newcastle-upon-Tyne, England – December 2004

"I know how much compassion and help you give to people. May you continue to be as open and as loving as you are now? Just looking at your webpage calms me down. May you go from strength to strength with your Angel Workshops?"
Your friend from across the Pond
Melinda Johns
Seattle, Washington, USA – September 2003

"Hi Ann, had a wonderful evening at your Angel Workshop and look forward to the next one at the end of the year. I had a look at the website – it is great and I am going to enjoy visiting it every now and then. Thanks."
Angeline McCaul
Cobh, Co. Cork, Ireland – May 2002

"Good Luck Ann with your Angel Workshops. I will be at the next one. Keep up the good work.
Love and Light."
Martina O'Flaherty
Cobh, Co. Cork, Ireland – May 2002

Colors: Archangels

Colors representing some of the Archangels:

Gabriel	Green
Raphael	Blue
Michael	Red
Uriel	Earth Tones
Camael	Gold – Yellow – Red
Sandalphon	Greens – Sea-blues
Jophiel	Yellow
Raguel	Fawns – Browns – Creams
Cassiel	Russets Reds – Orange – Brown
Zadkiel	Dark Blue – Silver
Raziel	Purple
Haniel	Silver – Gold
Barakiel	Silver – Blues – Reds

The Astral Planes of Existence
Lord Maitreya
in the
(Office of the Christ)

There are 12 strands of DNA.

Monad	11 DNA
Spiritual Triad	10 DNA
Δ	9 DNA
The Soul	8 DNA
Incarnated Personality	7 DNA
4–Body System	6 DNA
Physical – Etheric – Astral	5 DNA
Mental and Spiritual	4 DNA
EARTH	3 DNA
Archangel Sandalphon	2 DNA
Earth Mother	1 DNA
Pan	
Mineral, Vegetable & Animal Kingdoms	

In many of the olden writings and teachings they say there are 7 Planes of Existence. The same number as the veiled layers in heaven you will move through, once you return to the spirit world and are fully back in your spirit essence.

The same number as the colors of the rainbow.

The same number as the Crystal Towers of Atlantis.

The first book deals briefly with the 1st 2nd and 3r Planes of Existence. A lot of information has been written about them and there is great deal of data and detail to take on board. There are also many areas to explore within the astral world and this book only covers a small part of the Astral Plane of Existence. (The Mental and the Divine Planes of Existence are dealt with in Books 2 and 3). Maybe the fun, in all of this, will be in the exploring of the Angel Realms, as you connect with the Angels.

The Physical – is where we live:

It is the 1st Plane of Creation. Words describe the physical plane as being impenetrable, the thickest and the heaviest of the 7 Planes. The earth is a dense (heavy) world in which your souls live within the physical body; thus allowing you to move around more freely. Learning the lessons you are here to learn.

Esoteric teachings (meanings) can be extremely complex. To be honest, I found a lot of it went over my head. So I will put it as simply as I can and in layman's terms.

> *"It is a plane other than the physical; it is*
> *formed as a higher state of consciousness that*
> *transcends the universe as we know it."*

I hope I have not baffled you too much.

The Astral – is also our world:

It is the 2nd Plane of Creation and is more intricate and detailed. It is the world in which the animal, mineral and vegetable kingdoms reside. The Archangel Sandalphon rules the 7th Heaven and under the protection and guardianship of Lord Maitreya in the Office of the Christ; Sandalphon is the Ruling Angel and Protector of the Earth.

He is the Angel who hears and takes your prayers to God.

All prayers and requests are heard and acted upon.

Archangel Sandalphon is a tall Angel, an Angel of Mercy and a Master of Music. He is the protectorate of the Guardian Spirit. Early sources refer to Sandalphon as having been incarnated on earth as The Prophet Elijah. He is said to carry a wooden staff symbolising knowledge and wisdom. He was elevated into an Archangel by God; (though some sources say that this is unlikely).

Ancient writings say that Sandalphon was charged with anchoring the light onto the earth. As he works with the light-workers, he will help you to anchor your own light to the earth if you ask him; thus enabling you to become conduits of light-energy for the planet and to bring harmony and balance into your body.

His name means Messiah.

The fragrances and oils of lily, ivy or willow will help you to connect to the Archangel Sandalphon in meditation. In (midrashic) and other writings Sandalphon is described as the twin brother of Metatron the King of the Angels. Metatron was said to have incarnated on earth as Enoch in human origin.

The Mayan Calendar is on count down to the 21st December 2012 and the Archangel Sandalphon in co-operation with Sanat Kumara (and other Ascended Masters) will oversee the ascension phrase and the initiations in the inner planes.

Sanat Kumara is the Planetary Logos and has an ascension seat in Shambhalla over the Gobi Desert where you may ask to go in meditation or sleep. Sanat Kumara is the greatest of the Avatars. He is the Ruler of this Universe.

The Ascended Masters; Saint Germaine (who brought the Violet Flame of Purification and is now the Lord of Civilization) and the Master El Morya, Chohan of The First Ray are working together towards the Great Shift into the fifth-dimension.

With Lady Portia one of the Lords of Karma; Melchizedek an Ancient Cosmic Being and Commander Ashtar of the Intergalactic Fleet, they are here to help humanity regain their trust and belief and help you reconnect to the Divine Source.

Archangel Sandalphon brings the ancient teachings, knowledge and wisdom that has been held in safe-keeping since the Fall of Atlantis.

The Watchers are already here on the earth, waiting in the shadows, to take up their positions when the Great Shift of higher consciousness into the fifth-dimension begins.

History – Legend – Myth?

It will be a time of discovery when the 13 Crystal Skulls of Atlantis are found; a time when humanity has need of them the most and when you will be ready, once again to receive these powers and use them wisely.

Many and varied hypotheses have said the 13 crystal skulls are the legacy of a higher consciousness or ancient-beings who brought life to the earth in the race of humanity.

Into all the great mysteries of life, death and rebirth, tales and stories have been woven in the fabric of time, that once the 13 crystal skulls (hidden on earth) are placed in their rightful position within the Circle of Light – The Circle of Life – the secrets of the earth will be revealed.

Access to the secrets of the earth, will be through the Archangel Sandalphon (and other Ascended Masters) who have been entrusted to bring the ancient insight back to human-kind but:

Are you ready?

Are you worthy to receive these secrets once they are passed on?

Are you capable of understanding what it is all about?

The Angels ask little, except that you are vigilant and caring in your relationship with the earth. That you learn to live more closely and in tune with the planet; and you really care for the environment.

Changes are coming; changes to shape your life and your

future. The reality you are living in now is changing; shifting into a higher consciousness – a new state of awareness, as you enter the fifth-dimension.

This IS going to happen.

No matter what humanity says or does.

How traumatic this will be is dependent to a large extent on each of you. Humanity has free will, which is based on belief, religion, views and opinions. You also have the ability if you have the courage to see what is waiting for you, to grab it in both hands and set sail on a smooth and safe passage into the golden age of new beginnings.

Within all the ancient texts and writings, it all boils down to a simple-held belief of faith and trust. To do what feels right for you, in order for you to accept it.

This simple belief can be said of the World of Elementals and the Fairies that live in the nature gardens of the Astral Plane of Existence.

Do they exist?

The World of Elementals and Fairies
Do Fairies live at the bottom of the garden?

Earth: Gnomes – Elves – earth spirits – Satyrs
Small and mischievous
They dress in woodland greens, browns and russet reds
Old in appearance, grey-white hair and long beards
They look after the forests, woodlands, gardens and all things of nature

Air: Sylphs – air spirits
They have the highest vibratory rate of all the elementals and are the most beautiful
They are seen with wings and sometimes look like cherubs or fairies
Their job is to help humanity reach inspiration and creativity

Water: Undines – water spirits
They direct the flow and the course of the waters of the planet
Living in streams, ponds and beneath lily pads, they also inhabit the marshlands and waterfalls
Beautiful and emotional, the graceful Nature Spirits care for nature above and below the waters

Fire: Salamanders – spirits of fire
Salamanders help to keep you warm
They work through your emotions, bloodstream and liver
It is said a match cannot be lit, a fire cannot exist; without a salamander being present

They are the strongest and the most powerful of all the elementals

They help people who are friendly towards them

Salamanders have special powers over persons with fiery tempers

They will help the individual to keep their temper in check

The Casual is the 3rd Plane of Creation:

> Its medium is concrete – intellectual – energy
>
> It is Michael's plane of existence
>
> It contains the time track

Another way of saying, this is the area – place – region where energy fields reside; representing past and future experiences. It is said when you recall a past experience, you access the energy field of that experience.

It is called a memory.

Others say it is an experience that generates stronger energy fields which can be felt or sensed more than others; remembered better. Future experiences should be viewed only as possibilities; not certainties. I believe we create our own future in the here and the now; as we bring it from the world of dreams into the world of reality and by visualising it, we can make it our own.

The other 4 Planes of Existence will be dealt with in:

Angel Book 2:   The 4th – Akashic Plane

                    The 5th – Mental Plane

Angel Book 3:   The 6th – Messianic Plane

                    The 7th – Divine Plane

Angelic Ray Key: Angels and Color

The Angels I have listed below are the Angels of the Rays of Light and they represent the colors of the rainbow (and the colors of the chakras as well) – (red, orange, yellow, green, blue, indigo and violet). The rainbow is the combination of all these colors working together. Take a look at the chart and see which color suits you best. Which color is the most challenging and why?

Archangel Michael	Red
Archangel Uriel	Orange
Archangel Jophiel	Yellow
Archangel Raphael	Green
Archangel Gabriel	Indigo
Archangel Zadkiel	Violet
Mary-el Blue	(the angelic persona of Mother Mary Queen of the Universe and of Angels)

Every human being has a Guardian Angel, who is assigned to them for all the lives they live. In meditation or in quiet reflection, you can connect to your Guardian Angel and ask them their name. In doing so, you will find you have gained a whole new family; a team of Angels who work with you and for you. Have you met yours?

Do not search for us we will find you

Do not wait for us, we are here… already

Do not whisper your name, we know it well

We have loved you forever, time will tell…

We are your Guardian Angels

I hope you have enjoyed reading the first book on your journey into the amazing world of Angels, as much as I have enjoyed writing it.

I look forward to you joining me again, as you continue with your journey, along the pathway to love and enlightenment.

Special Thanks and Acknowledgements

To the Angels who walk at my side. Thank you for being there and for giving me the courage and help to write the first book. To my Spirit Guide Bear Running; thank you for your love and support. To all the wonderful authors, whose books I have read and learnt from, which has enabled me to gain valuable understanding and experience; as I walk my own pathway to spiritual truth and enlightenment.

Silver Birch [1]   Page 32-33
E W Wallis [2]   Page 35
Gautama Buddha [3]   Page 75

To Jeanetta for the wonderful talks we shared and for the insight you helped me to find especially the Planes of Existence, which I teach to the participants who attend the Angel Workshops. The love and light of this up-lifting and inspirational information, reaches out to all who want to learn and to know more about the Angelic Hierarchy.

My sincere thanks and appreciation to the Spiritualist Churches and venues where I have been invited to teach and run the Angel Workshops and where I have served the Churches as a Rostrum Medium and demonstrator.

Across the Irish Sea to Cobh, Co. Cork, in Southern Ireland
Christian Spiritualist Church, Douglas in the Isle of Man
Altrincham, Ellesmere Port and the Wirral
Paranormal Investigations in Cheshire
Coffee Aroma in Birkenhead
Liscard Spiritualist Church in Wallasey

St. Helens Community Centre, the
Psychic Truth (Parkfield) and the
Liverpool Holistic Circle, Rosicrucian
Chapter AMORC in Liverpool
The Spiritualist Church in Holywell, North Wales
Farnworth Christian Spiritualist Church in Bolton
Runcorn Spiritualist Church in Cheshire
Waterloo Community Centre and All Things Holistic at the
Waterloo College, Sing Centre in Merseyside

To the Churches and people who have helped guide me: Daulby Street in Liverpool where my spiritual development first began. The Psychic Truth (Parkfield), Liverpool where I took my first Church Service with Tommy Richardson as my Chairperson.

Runcorn Spiritualist Church has always felt like home, from the moment I first walked through the doors in 1982. It is the Church I always come home to; the Church where I have shared happy memories and wonderful moments with Lynn Brookes, Joan and Diane and others.

The Independent Spiritualist People's Church in Birkenhead – known affectionately as Joseph's Church, it is a wonderful place filled with happy memories and amazing times that I spent with Nancy and Joseph.

To Dales Christian Spiritualist Church in Darley Dale – special thanks. It is always a pleasure to visit whenever I am in Derbyshire and to Altrincham, Birkenhead, Farnworth, Fenton, Stretford and Rock Ferry for giving me the opportunity to have served the Church.

Sincere thanks to the Christian Spiritualist Church in Duke Road, Douglas on the Isle of Man. Especially to Brenda and Malcolm, Ken and his partner John and all the other church members who have made me feel so welcome and wanted.

I have been serving this wonderful Church for many years and I look forward to serving it for many more years to come. I'm looking forward to my next trip to the island this coming November and also to the bookings made for 2013.

Last but not least, my sincere thanks and love to Carol Oakes (and her husband Dave) who have looked after me in their B&B Hotel on my visits to the island; when serving the Church. Also when I came over on holiday with my friend Ann. Carol you are a wonderful friend; thank you for opening up your home and for making me feel so welcome.

You make the most beautiful cards that I buy for my family and friends, for their birthdays and Christmas. They are absolutely thrilled with the lovely cards I give them; that are produced with your love and time.

I was told many years ago by a wonderful lady I met in Derbyshire named Dorothy that I would never have to advertise the Angel Workshops and this has proved to be true. The Angel Workshops are advertised by word of mouth, my reputation and name and they seem to fly across the world.

Saint Germaine and my Angels have also told me that the Angel Workshops will go from strength to strength and there will be future invites from around the world: New Zealand, Canada, Northern Ireland, USA, The Orient, Switzerland, Spain, Australia and Austria; plus many other wonderful countries and places.

So here's to you joining me along the way.

'A Promise Not Forgotten'

After my father passed in February 1987; numb with grief and in deep pain I wanted to find a place of peace and solace for myself; a quiet space where no one could find or bother me. I was living in a grotty one-roomed bed-sit and somehow I needed the time to find myself but I didn't know how or where to start.

During my lunch hour, I would walk across the road from my workplace to sit in the peace and silence of the Metropolitan Roman Catholic Cathedral which stood opposite the Everyman Theatre. In the quiet stillness of that precious hour, it gave me the strength to fight my grief and loneliness before going back to work. At that time I was crying into the blackness that was engulfing me; for a light to guide the way.

Since my mid-teens I had been interested in spiritualism; it was like a call to the unknown, an invisible bond that was always there; though just out of reach and when friends and work colleagues spoke of a Spiritualist Church in Aigburth, I felt as though a beacon of light had been lit during those dark bleak times.

The Spiritualist Church was called The Psychic Truth (Parkfield) and on a Wednesday evening I went to the open circle. I had been told all would be welcome; you could walk in off the street, regardless of religion or belief. The meeting lasted for an hour and a half and for that time no one could hurt me, no one could bother me; no one could find me.

In the semi-dimness I was alone with my pain and grief of losing my beloved father. Week after week I attended, each time finding the quietness I so desperately needed. At one or two of the evenings a medium would give me a message but for the most part I was left in quiet solitude as I worked through the anger and grief.

A regular medium at the Church was a man called Tommy Richardson, dark-haired and dark-eyed with a fiery disposition. One Wednesday evening, after I had been attending the open circle for some months, he gave me a message that I had the gift whatever that meant. At the time I had no idea what he was talking about.

So I listened politely, nodding or shaking my head where I thought appropriate, then I went home and promptly forgot what he had said. So you can imagine my surprise and shock on arriving at the Church early the following week and settling myself on a seat, I watched as a lady approached me just before the meeting began to tell me I had the gift.

Again I was not too sure what she had meant so I asked.

The lady's name was Joan and she explained that I could hear and see spirit and had done so since childhood. I must admit to finding the matter rather amusing and so I didn't take her seriously, but she was not put out in the slightest by my disbelief and said I would be given proof; then she went to sit down.

Over the next few months, I became more and more aware of the strange and inexplicable happenings but like the proverbial ostrich I stuck my head firmly in the sand. After one evening at the Church and having been impressed with the messages Tommy had given me, I decided to have a one-to-one reading with him and in May of 1987 I went to see him.

As I left the house, I found I had more butterflies in my stomach than usual and I arrived at the Church in Parkfield earlier than I had intended. During the reading Tommy told me about my father and what the family had placed in his coffin; 3 red roses, a small oasis of flowers that my sister and I had put in, and the loaf.

Tommy told me many personal things he couldn't possibly have known. He told me that one day in the future I would be doing what he was doing. I would be working as a Rostrum Medium. He said my father was in the room and described him in great detail and how there had been no time to say goodbye, and the poem that had been written.

I was at a very low point in my life, my father had died and although at the time I didn't know it, I would lose my mother a few months later, so there was no way on God's little green earth I could ever have seen myself as a medium, let alone working as one, but Tommy was insistent it would happen. Nodding my head here and there to appease him, I left the Church after my reading and went home and put what he had said right out of my mind.

Thirteen years later as I walked up to the Rostrum to take my first Church Service at The Psychic Truth (Parkfield) in Liverpool, as a working medium; I saw Tommy Richardson waiting for me.

He had kept his promise.

Oh didn't I tell you, at that first reading with him thirteen years earlier, Tommy had made a promise that when I took my first Church Service he would take it with me.

Spirit had not forgotten and neither had he.

A promise that had been made, so many years ago, had been kept.

At that moment I knew Spirit walked with me, for if they could keep a promise made over a decade before, how could I not trust them unconditionally.

No Time To Say Goodbye

Sitting by your bedside
Your hand clasped tight in mine
Deep in sleep I watch
As your restless soul takes flight
Endless tossing and turning
Time is drawing nigh
Your spirit reaches out
Into the darkness of time

My heart is full of sorrow
My thoughts are filled with hope
Never again to see your smiling face
Or hear your laughing voice
Be able to walk with you; sit with you
Would be more than my heart can take

The long night is painful and lonely
As you fight every step of the way
It's a fight you can't hope to win
As you stand before Heaven's gate
Although you no longer know me
Or even that I am there
I sit beside your bedside
And watch you slumber
Deeper into God's loving care

But a moment in time is still with me
When you turned upon your side
Worth all of the waiting; not knowing
As you held my hand tight in yours
Is the smile that you gave me?
So warm and so loving
Your eyes shining brightly with love
And just for a second, one glorious second
Your beautiful brown eyes light up

Our time together is growing shorter
I selfishly want you to stay
Yet I know you would only suffer
If you where to remain here with me
The hours are passing so quickly
Time is no longer there

Beckoning you swiftly; silently
To return to your other world
I leave you but for a moment
A moment was all that it took
God welcomed you into his Kingdom
My world was no longer there

Looking down on your sleeping features
Your face no longer filled with pain
You've stepped once more
Into your other room
A room where I cannot see you
Yet I know you are still there
My eyes are filled with tears
As I tenderly kiss you goodbye
A whisper, a look; a silent moment
Goodnight; my Beloved Father sleep tight

Lightning Source UK Ltd.
Milton Keynes UK
UKOW050336230213

206704UK00001B/97/P